GOD LOVES YOU THIS MUCH

A STORY OF LOVE, LOSS, AND LEANING INTO JESUS

A Study of Ephesians

GOD LOVES YOU THIS MUCH-

Unless otherwise noted, Scripture quotations are from the *Holy Bible*, New International Version, © 1973, 1978, 1984 by International Bible Society. Used by permission

Scripture quotations marked NASB is from the *New American Standard Bible.* © The Lockman Foundation, 1960, 1962, 1963, 1968, 1971, 1972, 1973, 1975, 1977. Used by permission.

Scripture quotations labeled NLT are from the *Holy Bible*, New Living Translation, Copyright© 1996, 2004, 2015 by Tyndale House Foundation. Used by permission of Tyndale House Publishers, Inc., Carol Stream, Illinois 60188. All Rights Reserved.

Scripture quotations labeled KJV are from the King James Version of the Bible

Scripture quotations labeled AMP-CE are from the Amplified Bible, copyright © 1954, 1958, 1962, 1964, 1965, 1987 by The Lockman Foundation. Used by permission.

Scripture quotations labeled Message are from THE MESSAGE, Copyright © by Eugene H. Peterson 1993, 1994, 1995, 1996, 2000, 2001, 2002. Used by permission of Navpress. All Right Reserved. Represented by Tyndale House Publishers, Inc.

ISBN-13:978-1974292653
ISBN-10:1974292657

Dedication

This Bible study is dedicated to my loving Relevant Church family. May the Holy Spirit guide each of you into "all truth" that you may become all that Jesus desires for your life and your calling, for each of us are made to belong. May each of us truly know *God Loves Us This Much!*

Contents

As I studied the book of Ephesians, I was amazed at how God's story entwined with my life story. I felt compelled by the Spirit of God to share my story with others. The result was the creation of this Bible study with the intent of coinciding with my story, *God Loves You This Much*. My prayer is as you use this study guide God will show you how your own story is woven into God's story as well, and you allow His Spirit to move in you. I pray my life, and God's work in my life will be a healing ointment to the areas that are hurting and broken in your life. May God renew and refresh your faith journey through this time in His Word.

Sincerely,

Susie Wirth

Week One: My Song
Ephesians 1:1-14

Key Passage: This is What He Wanted to Do!
Ephesians 1:5 (NIV)

> **"⁵he predestined us to be adopted as his sons through Jesus Christ, in accordance with his pleasure and will"**

In the first chapter of my story, or if you have listened to the teaching segment, "My Song," I laid out for you the premise for this study. Truly this is an act of obedience to my loving God upon my part because I would never take this adventure on myself. It is simply not pleasurable to revisit all the trials and hurts from my past. As I try to share my story of wrestling with God through the hurts and losses in my life, I hope you will be encouraged and learn from the mistakes I have made. I pray God will do the healing work in your heart He so desperately wants to do; and I pray He will use His Word to transform your life for eternity.

Each week we will study a key passage taken from the book of Ephesians in conjunction with a part of my personal story. This week I pray you will receive the fact God chose you, and this is what He wants to do in each of our lives. This act of His love for you and me gives Him great pleasure. Ephesians 1:5 is our key passage this week. As we study together, may the Spirit of the living, loving God allow you to experience the fullness of His love for you - for how great is His love for you.

Day 1 A Letter to Me?
Read Ephesians 1:1 & 2

When we tackle a Bible study it is important to see the study from a holistic viewpoint. One of the greatest commentaries and Bible teachers of our modern age writes of Ephesians:

"The Epistle to the Ephesians is a complete Body of Divinity. In the first chapter you have the doctrines of the gospel; in the next, you have the experience of the Christians; and before the Epistle is finished, you have the precepts of the Christian faith. Whosoever would see Christianity in one treatise, let him read, mark, learn, and inwardly digest the Epistle to the Ephesians."[1]

So, as we study verse-by-verse, chapter-by-chapter, let us keep in mind this letter holds so much for us to learn. Let us take the necessary time to consume all we possibly can digest!

We read this letter's salutation and know a man named Paul is the writer. However, Paul is no ordinary man! His testimony permeates the New Testament. No other person may ever match the Apostle Paul's boldness and zeal for our Lord. We also understand he is writing to a group of "faithful followers" in a seaport town named Ephesus. But who are these people and why was this letter written? These were followers of Jesus. They believed what this strange and foreign man had told them years earlier about the story of Jesus. They believed and are now called not just followers of Jesus, but "faithful" followers of Jesus. The Apostle Paul is an intricate part of this study, but this is not a study of Paul. There are many Bible resources where you can read more about the life and ministry of the Apostle Paul, and I encourage you to do so.

If you were to receive a letter from a church leader, how would you expect your salutation to read? Would you be called a follower? In our culture, one would most likely be addressed by a first name if well known to the church leader. The content would most likely be some kind of formal communication, since the technological revolution of our social communication through Facebook, Twitter, and texting have almost taken the place of letter writing.

More important than the salutation of this Biblical letter, is the reason for the letter. This was the only means by which Paul could encourage the followers in Ephesus! There was no face-time, internet access, web cameras, or instant messages in those days!

Think about the arrival of this letter. Would the followers of Jesus be excited? How might they react? How do you react when you receive a letter in the mail? For me, there is a specific, undeniable feeling that accompanies the written word. Yet, I have a conflict about writing emails; on many occasions, I have said: "How I hate writing emails, especially ones that may be of a negative nature." You just cannot determine the writer's tone, inflections, or even emotions. In person, face-to-face conversation gives both people an advantage in the interpretation of body language and facial expression. Yet this is not how God has given us His Word. We have a written Word, and we are responsible for allowing the Spirit to guide us into all truth and understanding. I believe this is exactly what is meant by John 16:13.

> "Howbeit when he, the Spirit of truth, is come, he will guide you into all truth: for he shall not speak of himself; but whatsoever he shall hear, that shall he speak: and he will show you things to come." (KJV)

Now, imagine what it must have been like for this early group of believers to receive a letter from the Apostle Paul. Write down why you believe these words of encouragement would have been so important?

_____

_____

_____

If you were one of those early followers of Jesus, explain how the word "faithful" would have made you feel?

_____

_____

_____

Re-read John 16:13. What is God speaking to you about through this passage of Scripture?

12

_____

_____

_____

What current hurts are you holding onto and how is the Spirit of God speaking to your heart?

_____

_____

_____

Day 2 The Blessing
Read Ephesians 1:3

In reading this verse, did you skim through all of the hoopla of praise and glory like I did? I mean, what is the big deal? Why do the writers of the Bible seem to be jumping up and down all of the time? Ok, I know I sound harsh and ungrateful, but really…. in my realm of reality - the here and now - I have a "to do" list a mile long, a messy house, and quite frankly I am not in the mood to be at a cheer-fest! Yes, and my YouVersion on my smart phone has lost its connection!

Do you ever feel like me? Sometimes it seems the Word has so little to do with my world.

Let us stop and think about the cause of this praise and celebration. At first glance, the blessings I have received, while appreciated, do not necessarily or immediately make me want to get excited and praise God. Shame on me! (I bet you all are fully disgusted with me already.) What are these spiritual blessings mentioned in this verse and why do they elicit such a response? I was so curious I looked up their meaning in the Greek. What I came up with was more praise. However, this time I found myself becoming a bit more interested when I noticed it was a blessing of praise spoken from God Himself through the Spirit! This is much like how a father would speak a "blessing" upon his child. If this is really what is meant, then my attention is quickened and I am now eager, not bored, to hear a spiritual blessing from God as my Father, blessing me as His child! I mean, who wouldn't be?

I know the times in my life when my earthly father has spoken blessings to me; these words became cherished. They were so great I have never forgotten those sweet words. They were words that remind me of who I am and what I can accomplish. When I am feeling less than adequate, those blessed words come back to me and encouraged me!

Words are so powerful, whether we want to admit it or not. Still, we have not only been given spiritual blessings verbally, the way God has "blessed" us is significant as well. This word "blessed" is in the verb tense meaning action. This is a direct action from God. That thought ought to make me turn my attention from myself to consider more intently this meaning of being "blessed" by God. It means God "invokes this upon me." Not just a group of faithful believers from the town of Ephesus, but also little ole' me! He bestows them on you as well, if you are a faithful follower of Jesus Christ! Even in the Old Testament, when the words "hath blessed" were used, it meant a great deal. Whoever was the recipient could expect to prosper, to be happy, and to have blessings bestowed upon them. No wonder there is so much excitement written from the Apostle Paul! He is proclaiming to these faithful followers "they are blessed by God!" An authenticated, God-breathed, Spiritual…Father God BLESSING!!!

Can you recall a blessing your father, mother, or any person in authority – a grandparent, pastor, teacher has spoken over you? What was it and how has it affected your life?

_____

_____

_____

How does knowing God has "blessed" you and you are a recipient of spiritual blessings make you feel? Is it easier to understand why The Apostle Paul was so emphatically excited and calling for Praise to God?

_____

_____

_____

Day 3 He Chose Me!
Read Ephesians 1:4-8

As we studied yesterday, the spiritual blessings are very significant to the follower of Jesus. Each time "hath blessed" in the Old Testament was used, the phrase is followed by God's favor and good things. Who would not want "good things?"

Since we all would love "good things" in our lives, today we are going to examine these spiritual blessings and what they mean to us personally. Let us consider the first spiritual blessing bestowed upon the follower of Jesus Christ, which I believe is the most significant of all blessings.

It is the blessing of "sonship."

We have been chosen. Enough said. With the simple little phrase "you have been chosen by God" we could close our little study and go home. Being chosen, instead of being left on the playing field unwanted and rejected, is so significant to our human psyche. For those of us who have been rejected, looked over, or left on the playground of life in humiliation, the damaging idea of rejection is wiped away by the idea that God has chosen us! Take heart, God has chosen you, too!

Not only have we been chosen, selected out among others, the next verse, "to be blameless in His sight," carries a whole other meaning. You see, it carries with it the truth we have direct access to the presence and community of God. "How?" one may ask. Since we have been made blameless before Him, God our Father, through the work of Jesus on the cross, we can now enter His fellowship. Or God's Holy presence! Before being made blameless, I guess you could say we were "to blame?" With blame or any part of sin, so, God could not be in our presence because HE is HOLY and thus, we could never be in His presence. Yet, through the spiritual blessing of being chosen, we can be with God forever.

Yet we are not just left with being able to access God Himself. As if that were not enough, in verse 5 we see that God loved us so much He decided in advance to adopt us! Catch this thought and ponder it a moment, God did not wait until He met us or looked upon us, but He loved us so much that He had predetermined long before we were a twinkle in our parents' eyes that He wanted us as His own children!

One commentator explains the significance of "adoption into God's family this way:

This high position in the family of God gives us something in Jesus that Adam never had. "When people ask us the speculative question why God went ahead with the creation when he knew it would be followed by the fall, one answer we can tentatively give is he destined us for a higher dignity than even creation would bestow on us."[2]

Wow! God loves us this much! It was our destiny to be adopted into His family. It is our position to have dignity!

Let us consider adoption for a few moments longer. I know many families that have gone through the adoption process, and it is a very difficult road. The process is long and complicated. Adoption is always a sacrifice in some way or another. I cannot help but think the adopting parents love must grow and deepen through the arduous task of adopting. Just like legal adoptions today, the road to our spiritual adoption was long and complicated. It took God in Heaven giving up His beloved Son Jesus to come to earth, become a lowly baby, grow, live, and then go to the cross. This is our ultimate example of unconditional and sacrificial love. Oh, how the Father's love is toward us!

List below the first two spiritual blessings:

a. _____

b. _____

He **chose** me to be blameless before Him, so I could enter into His presence and talk to Him. He made my destiny before time began, to be **adopted** into His family and to be His child, an heir of royal blood and lineage. And if those two were not enough, our third spiritual blessing is the most incredible of all.

We are accepted because we are **forgiven**!!!

Free from the dread of guilt and the shame that I so deservingly should bear! The Psalmist states, "Our sin is as far as from the East is to the West!" (Psalm 103:12) and means. He remembers them no more! This alone is an awesome thought

The great news is He chose you too! John 3:16 states "For God so loved the world that he gave his one and only Son, that whoever believes in Him should not perish but have eternal life." Whoever means He chose you too!

Have you chosen Him? If so, what does it mean to you to be chosen of God?

_____

_____

_____

How does it make you feel that you are not only chosen by God but chosen for God to be His child, a royal heir with a royal destiny and royal access to the King of Kings and Lord of Lords?

_____

_____

_____

The Bible also states, "If we confess our sins and believe on what Jesus did on the cross, we can be saved." (Romans 10:10) Some may question, SAVED from what? The Word of God is clear that all have sinned and come short of the glory or perfection of God. We have missed perfection and carry the weight and guilt of our sins unless we confess our sins and believe in the work Jesus did on the cross to relieve us of our debt for that sin. Then and only then can we be forgiven and be a follower of Jesus Christ, and thus a recipient of the spiritual blessings bestowed upon us.

Have you ever asked God for forgiveness? Have you ever confessed you believe Jesus is God's son and died for you?

_____

_____

_____

To be a follower of Jesus one must be a believer of who Jesus is and what He did. In the following blanks please explain why you believe you can call yourself a follower of Jesus?

_____

_____

_____

There is yet another Spiritual Blessing we don't want to miss! In verse 8, we see spiritual blessings with the showering of God's kindness upon us. Our next blessing is the kindness of our Father through all wisdom and understanding.

That is a huge chunk of God's Word to chew upon, but as you consider the magnitude of this blessing, what does it mean to you that God has showered you with His kindness and all wisdom and understanding?

_____

_____

_____

In conclusion, I want us to note that spiritual blessings are not just confined to these passages. There are numerous spiritual blessings throughout Scripture. Still, I love how Charles Spurgeon commented on these particular passages. He states,

"Our thanks are due to God for all temporal blessings; they are more than we deserve. But our thanks ought to go to God in thunders of hallelujahs for spiritual blessings. A new heart is better than a new coat. To feed on Christ is better than to have the best earthly food. To be an heir of God is better than being the heir of the greatest nobleman. To have God for our portion is blessed, infinitely more blessed than to own broad acres of land. God hath blessed us with spiritual blessings. These are the rarest, the richest, the most enduring of all blessings; they are priceless in value."[3]

Yes, and amen!

Day 4 The Plan
Read Ephesians 1:9-11

Whether we categorize this plan as a spiritual blessing or not, the "plan" is obviously a new revelation to these faithful followers of Jesus. The Apostle Paul even goes so far as to call this plan a mystery. Amazingly, God let us in on His previously hidden plan! Not only the plan of our destiny but also the destiny of the entire world. The Heavens and the Earth. The grandest plan in Heaven and on Earth! So, what is this plan? In the space below write down what you believe this grand plan entails.

_____

_____

_____

Today many believers have been taught from childhood Jesus is our Savior, and that He died, rose from the dead, and went up into the Heavens to prepare a place for us. And, most pertinent to our lesson today, Jesus is going to return to the earth again someday. I can even think of countless songs that have the phrase, "Jesus is coming again…" Yet if we consider these early followers, they had not heard much about Jesus' return other than the fact His last words to the Galatians standing on the hillside when Jesus was taken up into the Heavens were, and I am paraphrasing, Why are you still standing here staring… this same Jesus that was taken up into Heaven will come again in the same way. (Acts 1:11)

So, as far as they were concerned, they only knew that Jesus would come again. These early followers were probably thinking Jesus would come back in a few days or a week and set up His Kingdom so they could be free right then and in their lifetimes. The Apostle Paul seems to be urging them to consider more than just their place here on Earth as followers of Jesus Christ, but to also consider the over-arching plan of the ages, their future, and what place they had personally in this plan. Prefaced with the blessings of all knowledge and understanding, these followers can be assured at the right time God will bring everything in Heaven and Earth together under the authority of Christ. This unifying or bringing together is vitally important because it means all the wrongs will be righted. It means we have hope from our losses. It sums up what Romans 8:18-22 expresses:

Romans 8:18-22 (NIV)

"[18]I consider that our present sufferings are not worth comparing with the glory that will be revealed in us. [19]The creation waits in eager expectation for the sons of God to be revealed. [20]For the creation was subjected to frustration, not by its own choice, but by the will of the one who subjected it, in hope [21]that the creation itself will be liberated from its bondage to decay and brought into the glorious freedom of the children of God. [22]We know that the whole creation has been groaning as in the pains of childbirth right up to the present time."

And he reminds us again it is because we are united with Christ and heirs, thus receiving an inheritance, that everything will work together according to this grand plan.

David Guzak, Bible Commentator expresses this great plan this way, "Having made known to us the mystery of His will: Part of what belongs to us under the riches of His grace is the knowledge of the mystery of His will, God's great plan and purpose which was once hidden but is now revealed to us in Jesus. Through the Apostle Paul, God calls us to consider the greatness of God's great plan for the ages and our place in that plan."[4]

So just as the Apostle Paul wanted those early followers to consider their purpose and understand all things in life are under the great "plan" of God, we too need to understand how this great "plan" directly affects us today.

Have you ever considered your life as part of a "greater plan"? Does this understanding appeal to any part of you? If so, write about what God is speaking to your heart.

_____

_____

_____

There is so much of Christian Doctrine in this first half of chapter one that I realize it can make for a dizzy head. Still, these truths are so important for the foundations God is laying in our lives through this study of healing and hope.

To sum up briefly what we have discovered about this mysterious plan of God:

    The plan will be initiated by God at just the right time.

    The plan gives God great pleasure.

The plan will be carried out by Jesus, the Son.

The plan will be under the authority of Jesus and even Heaven and Earth will be subject to this great plan.

This great plan gives us, as followers, a great inheritance.

I want so desperately for you to understand HOW this relates to you, right where you are today. Whether you are in a quiet place or tumultuous place, or maybe somewhere in-between those two places, God's great plan is for you. Without this full understanding of God's greater plan and our inheritance that is to come, we can easily fall prey to overwhelming circumstances when we experience losses in our lives. Truth gets buried in our grief and our emotions drown us in sorrow. Yet because of our HOPE in this great plan, our understanding that we will inherit life everlasting in Heaven with God and the truth all things including death and decay will come together "under the authority of Christ," we know our greatest losses on this earth will end in gain. We need to grasp firmly to our destiny and inheritance in times of great loss more than in times of peace and prosperity. I was reminded of these great truths yesterday as I attended a memorial for a baby that was stillborn. It was so beautiful to experience a large group of people honoring a life that only lived a brief time in the womb of his mother. To know that death and decay are going to be wiped out of our existence one day was the ONLY comfort. The Apostle Paul so desperately wanted these faithful followers to understand this great plan so they (and we) would understand the curse of this world is death, and part of the great "plan" of God is freedom from experiencing this overwhelming pain and grief, and we will one day be brought together with our loved ones who are in Heaven.

In the days to follow we will continue to learn and discover more about this great plan, and details will unfold as we seek to understand the truths of Scripture. Hang on friends; we have much to learn together!

Day 5 A Guarantee
Read Ephesians 1:12-14

What does the word "guarantee" mean to you? When looking for a used car recently we wanted to get a car with a warranty… but guarantee? Sometimes the phrase "I guarantee it" does not have much value in our world today. We were recently guaranteed school uniforms would be ready before school started. Guaranteed, until they were not ready. Then what? Well, we are over two weeks into school and still no uniforms. Unfortunately, our words do not carry much weight anymore. Still, there is a Word that carries much weight because it is faithful and true. The Word. When the Word of God is spoken, the idea of "yes, and amen" comes to my mind. Amen means "so be it!" or "It is so!" Not much in our world can be trusted to "be so" or remain true to its word. I guess that is why some, myself included, find it occasionally difficult to believe the Word.

When God doesn't answer on my timetable or according to my will, I find myself questioning. What about you? Do you ever question God? One of the greatest assurances found in the Bible is given in this passage. I love it because so many people struggle with the idea they CANNOT know for sure they are God's children. I realize this is a debated issue for some, but in my over 25 years of ministry, especially with counseling young people, the question that is most troubling is this: "How do I know I am truly a chosen child of God?"

For those of you that are sure of your position in the family of God, please be patient as we discuss such a vitally important question. Imagine, if you will, the place the enemy could take in our hearts and minds if we constantly questioned who we are in Christ. Write down some consequences that might occur if someone struggles with whether or not they are really a child of God or not.

_____

_____

_____

In verse 14, the Scripture states "who is a deposit guaranteeing our inheritance until the redemption of those who are God's possession--to the praise of his glory."

Here is our guarantee again. But think not of those words in earthly terms, because our God is faithful, tried and true. He cannot nor will He ever change, according to Hebrews 13:8. "Jesus Christ is the same yesterday, and today, and forever." (NIV)
And He cannot nor ever will He ever lie because He is Truth and He is Love and there is no error found in Him.

So bank on it... the guarantee that the Word speaks of here is secure and true! So instead of asking the question, "Am I a child of God?" – a better question is, "Do I have the Spirit?" Some evidence to look for to find the Spirit of God living in you are found in Galatians 5:21-23. Please take time right now to read this passage.

According to this passage of Scripture, how can we know if the Spirit of God is living in us?

_____

_____

_____

With young people, I often explain our spiritual relationship with God our Father this way: "Just like our earthly fathers may get upset, we are still their children and nothing we can do or say can take the DNA blood out of our veins and separate us. So is our relationship with our Heavenly Father, nothing we can do or say can separate us, once we are in Him and He, by His Spirit, is in us!"

God wants to work His perfect will and plan for our lives through us without us having any doubt or fear that somehow, we are not His children. This kind of fear only causes a wall between us. So, have this guarantee today: if you have believed in what Jesus did on the cross and asked Him to come into your heart and forgive you, you are a child of God - even when things come between you.

More on these verses later. As we study, we see an important reminder that the Apostle Paul wanted these followers, who were Gentile followers, to keep before them. A huge part of the plan of God was to include them into the family of God. Jews were first, but because of God's lavish love for all, even those who were considered pagans are now included in this mysterious plan of God. We miss the significance of this simple fact because we do not understand the enormity of this revelation in their culture! The only thing I can liken it to in our culture today would be the Muslim extremist accepting a Christian into his faith without requiring the Christian to embrace his tradition. Talk about counter cultural. Paul was preaching that Gentiles did not have to be circumcised in order to belong to Christ's family. I see this struggle culturally and it is often a point of argument in the Scriptures. Still we have our own cultural struggles and what we as a culture struggle with even more than believing God for our salvation is the fact the Gospel is almost too easy. I have found there are many who simply will not accept the gift of forgiveness Christ offers because they feel it is too easy. Do you believe the Gospel is easy?

_____

_____

_____

One final thought about our salvation is the word "seal" as found in the King James Version of these verses. This word is evidence we are marked with the Holy Spirit. We cannot undo this mark however hard we may try. This seal is a permanent position in Christ.

After studying this first half of chapter one of Ephesians, do you know who you are in Christ any better than you did when we first started our study adventure together?
If so, complete the phrases "I know who I am in Christ because

_____

_____

_____

How well do you feel you know yourself? Do you take time to reflect upon your life or is your life so busy you don't have time to even think about it?

_____

_____

_____

What about God? Does God have a place in your heart and life? Are you discovering He has a great plan for you? Describe your relationship.

_____

_____

_____

What is the worst thing that has ever happened to you in your life? Have you been able to see God through the tragedy?

_____

_____

_____

On a scale from 1-10 with 10 being you are fully recovered from it and 1 being you are still being rocked by it, rank where you feel you would be on the scale.

1----2----3----4----5----6----7----8----9----10

Week Two: Hope & Loss
Ephesians 1:15-23

Key Passage: Understand the Greatness of His Power
Ephesians 1:19-20 (NIV)

> **"[19]and his incomparably great power for us who believe. That power is like the working of his mighty strength, [20]which he exerted in Christ when he raised him from the dead and seated him at his right hand in the heavenly realms**"

In "My Story" I exposed my need of hope. If you have not already found your need of hope, there will be times in your life when you will be driven to it. Through Scripture we can understand our God is the God of ultimate power. In this divine power, we can derive the hope we need for any given situation in our lives. As we firm up our power source, I pray this sense of concrete power will be our source from which we find hope. Hope from the despair of our past, present, and even our future.

As we study together, may the Spirit of the living, loving God grant that you experience the fullness of God's love for you, for how great is His love for you. Be diligent in your studies this week, dear friend.

Day 1 A Constant
Read Ephesians 1:15 & 16

"You are my refuge and my shield; I have put my hope in your word." (Psalms 119:14)

What would it mean to have a constant friend? One who is reliable, faithful, and always available?

In these verses, we see an example of Christianity at its finest. The loving Apostle affirms to those followers in Ephesus he is constantly praying for them.

I know the people that are my constants. I can count them on my two hands, and I know whom I can call on for prayer in times of urgency. These are the people who pray for me constantly! It is almost impossible for me to explain how difficult it is to raise a mentally handicapped child. Yet knowing there are constants in my life, people who carry me through each day on the sweet whispers of prayer is a great comfort in times of need and in the simple days of the mundane. And believe me, there are many times a day when I have to re-arrange my thinking to focus on things above and NOT on things of this earth! I may not even talk to some of these dear family or friends for weeks at a time, yet I am confident they are there. They are praying. They are my constants!

Still, more than desiring for these early followers to know he is constantly praying for them, by declaring this prayer commitment on their behalf their spiritual leader, the Apostle Paul, wanted them to know again how proud he was of their strong faith in the Lord! He affirmed their faith once again as in the salutation of the letter.

None of us would want to say we are needy people. Has not society and culture trained us to be independent? Yet, I admit I absolutely love it when someone affirms me or edifies me. There is nothing like being lifted up and told, "Hey, you are doing a great job here!" And doesn't the encouragement have even more significance when it comes from someone you admire and respect? Well, in this passage of Scripture the founder of their body of believers the Apostle Paul, in the flesh, was saying, "Way to go!" "You are doing a great job with loving others!" And, "I am so proud of you!" In times of trouble or pain in our lives, we need others to surround us.

How does it make you feel when a person you respect encourages and affirms what you are doing? What are the effects of those powerful words on you?

_____

_____

_____

How might you encourage or affirm someone else today?

_____

_____

_____

Do you have a constant in your life? Who are the people you know are lifting you up in prayer daily?

_____

_____

_____

If you are struggling with not having a constant, why don't you find a friend that could be a prayer partner with you? Especially in times of hurt and despair, we need other people. Oftentimes the enemy will try to make us think we should keep to ourselves and get through the pain alone. This is just the opposite of what we should do! We need people that are going to give us sound Biblical advice. God never intended for any of us to walk this journey alone!

We are made to belong! In order for us to be a constant we need to really get to know other believers. Doing life in community is one way followers of Jesus can learn to pray for one another like our example, the Apostle Paul. What are your thoughts about the idea of doing life together with a community of believers?

_____

_____

_____

Do whatever is necessary to find a constant in your life and be a constant for someone else.

Day 2 God Wants Me To Grow
Read Ephesians 1:17-18

I know when I completed college and walked down the aisle of that institute of higher learning I felt a great sense of accomplishment. It was such a feeling of satisfaction that other events in my life cannot even come close to matching it. I also remember thinking to myself, "I will never have to study for another exam again!" However nice that may have sounded in my brain at the time, life is meant for learning. I may not take written examinations on a regular basis anymore, but is not our life journey full of tests? Yes, we all must admit we need to continue to learn in order to move, grow, and even simply keep up with technology! That is a challenge unless you have a techie husband as I do that syncs cell phones and fixes computer viruses for you. Okay, and a whole lot more! These verses in Ephesians challenge us to grow. Not just in social standings or cultural graces, but to "grow in our knowledge of God." (vs.17) Growing in our knowledge of God is not just for knowledge's sake, but also for our own development. For our own sakes, God wants us to have a little thing called "confidence!" Confidence IN hope and confidence OF hope! Confidence in the knowledge we have attained! First, confidence in who we are in Christ, our hope of eternal glory; and second, confidence of our future inheritance. Yes, the confidence of our hope is a huge deal.

Why do you think it would be so important for us to understand knowledge about our future inheritance and have confidence in what we know to be true?

_____

_____

_____

Another idea about this "growing in the knowledge of God" is it comes through spiritual wisdom and insights straight from God! I find this so intriguing: the God of the Universe desires for me to gain spiritual wisdom and insights so I can know Him more. I just want to figure out how we can pick apart this spiritual wisdom and the insights from God that he really wants us to grasp! I do want to know Him more, don't you? There is much to understand about this striving, gaining, and knowing. So, let us continue studying.

We have established He indeed wants us to grow to know Him more. I believe this is the key to unlocking what is one of the most important spiritual precepts we can learn as a follower of

Christ. God knows our lives will be full of disappointments, losses, and even unspeakable grief. Yet, He so lovingly helps us along and grants us tools to do more than just "make it" in life. He wants us to know Him personally so we can be a light to others during our disappointments, losses, and grief.

Have you ever been at a place where even the thought of getting through the day was too much to consider? A place where just waking up and putting your feet on the floor seemed overwhelming? I have been there too. Because God knows us so well, God wants us to know Him so that we can rely on His faithful, unmovable, "constant" character because we need HIM. We need even more than to know about Him; we need to know Him in a personal way. Maybe you don't think you need Him now or at least this very second, but we all do need Him, and we grow now to rely on Him later. You see, if I know He is strong and His power is in me, I can rest upon His strength. "When I am weak…then I am strong." (2 Cor. 12:9-11 NLT)

Pick any character trait you need from God right now or may need in the future. God lives up to it and is the epitome of that trait. For example, let us use the word "faithful." Is there anyone so faithful as God? "Jesus Christ is the same yesterday and today and forever." (Heb. 13:8 KJV)

What about the character trait "love?" The Bible states, "God is love." (I Jn. 4:7&8 KJV) He is not just a lovable God, nor simply loving. Love is from Him and He IS love! Try picking any good character trait. I guarantee you our God is going to come out number one every time. I think we all must admit it is in the trials and struggles of life that we really need to know Him. I don't need God's comfort when all is well and life is great. I usually neglect Him (just being honest). But when life stinks He is the first to come to my rescue. If I didn't know that I know that I know Him, how could I trust Him with my life? A great exercise in knowing God more is to take a character trait each day and search the Scriptures to find how God lives up to that trait. He is trustworthy and reliable every single time. God not only wants us to call upon Him as a personal God in times of our greatest need, but He also wants to encourage us through those times. A relationship that is real goes both ways. We call upon Him and He responds.

It is your turn. Pick a character trait about God you need to know is true about Him and do your best to find a verse in the Bible that supports His character. Describe your search.

_____

_____

_____

In the last verse or our study today we talk about our great HOPE. This is what I find motivates me when I struggle.

What do you believe is the hope we are to be so confident of, spoken about in verse 18?

_____

_____

_____

Yes, I am hopeful one day this life with all of its disappointments, struggles, and loss will end and I will be ushered into a better place. Knowing with confidence this hope is an inheritance in Heaven someday, I can overcome any kind of disappointment, loss, or grief in this present life. And in this present life, knowing I have a loving, reliable, faithful, and strong Heavenly Father who will see me through the toughest of life's troubles allows me to walk confidently each and every day in knowing Him.

Take hope my friend and be confident in it today, for our God is our great hope.

Day 3 Our Source of Power
Read Ephesians 1:19-20

It is an amazing thing to consider that Jesus had the power to raise himself up from the dead. This belief is one no other religion on the face of the planet can claim. This fact separates faith in Christ Jesus from any other faith.

As we studied in the previous days, the imperative idea is to know God and hope in Him throughout our entire lives - whether in gain or loss. Today our focus is on knowing the resurrection power that seems so elusive and magical. This prayer from the Apostle Paul for the followers of Ephesus and for us today is we not only know God and hope in our future, but also that we understand, "His great power for us who believe."

In reading the passages list a few things we can know about this "power" which the Apostle Paul is describing.

_____

_____

_____

In my religious circles, I don't recall hearing a lot about the power of God, other than it was God's power. Here the text clearly teaches the power is the same mighty power God used to raise Christ from the grave and that the power is for "us" who believe.

So, does that mean I can tap into the power of the Almighty? And not just that power, but also the resurrection power of the Almighty, becoming a "super hero" here on earth?

I sincerely doubt it. So just what does this verse that is "for us" mean? I like to read several versions of the Scriptures when I am on a search, so I have chosen the Amplified Bible for today because it is very descriptive and exhaustive.

> "[17][For I always pray to] the God of our Lord Jesus Christ, the Father of glory, that He may grant you a spirit of wisdom and revelation [of insight into mysteries and secrets] in the [deep and intimate] knowledge of Him, [18]By having the eyes of your heart flooded with light, so that you can know and understand the hope to which He has

called you, and how rich is His glorious inheritance in the saints (His set-apart ones), [19]And [so that you can know and understand] what is the immeasurable and unlimited and surpassing greatness of His power in and for us who believe, as demonstrated in the working of His mighty strength, [20]Which He exerted in Christ when He raised Him from the dead and seated Him at His [own] right hand in the heavenly [places], [21]Far above all rule and authority and power and dominion and every name that is named [above every title that can be conferred], not only in this age and in this world, but also in the age and the world which are to come." (Ephesians 1:17-21 AMP)

Some key thoughts:

His power is A Mighty Resurrection strength- grade power!

His power cannot be measured!

His power is limitless!

His power surpasses all others in Heaven and Earth!

His power is IN us by the indwelling of His Holy Spirit!

His power is FOR us!

So, tap into the power source. Go ahead, but understand this power is not as easily grasped as one would assume.

Philippians 3:10 gives a little more insight into the "power."

"[10][For my determined purpose is] that I may know Him [that I may progressively become more deeply and intimately acquainted with Him, perceiving and recognizing and understanding the wonders of His Person more strongly and more clearly], and that I may in that same way come to know the power outflowing from His resurrection [[a]which it exerts over believers], and that I may so share His sufferings as to be continually transformed [in spirit into His likeness even] to His death, [in the hope]
[11]That if possible I may attain to the [[b]spiritual and moral] resurrection [that lifts me] out from among the dead [even while in the body].
[12]Not that I have now attained [this ideal], or have already been made perfect, but I press on to lay hold of (grasp) and make my own, that for which Christ Jesus (the Messiah) has laid hold of me and made me His own." (AMP, Philippians 3:10-12)

No, I don't believe we are super heroes in the making here on earth. I don't want to be so bold as to say a human has never raised another human in our modern age from the dead either. What I believe the Apostle Paul is saying in these two passages is, "we will be raised from death of this life and body, to life in Christ Jesus eternally." The power is in us for this to come to fruition when our appointed time arrives.

This is our great hope: Strength from God as we go through life's pains, hope for a better future, and power to be raised from death unto life eternal with God in Heaven one day.

It would be fun to be a super hero for God for a day. I admit it!

What would you do first?

_____

_____

_____

What is the Spirit of God speaking to your heart about today? If you have questions, go ahead and write them down.

_____

_____

_____

Day 4 God Above All
Read Ephesians 1:21

God above all! God is ranked above the greatest leader of all time. He will be better than any king to come. Thank God for that! Think of the greatest leader in human history. None can even come close to our God.

The passage states, "He is above humankind," but I believe it refers to all powers. What about Mother Nature? God created the Earth, so He is certainly above and greater than the power of the wind. He rules the seismic shifts and enormous forces of our solar system. A few years ago, we experienced what NASA called the biggest Solar Radiation Storm since 2003. No one remembered the headlines in the next week because only a few polar flights were diverted due to possible communication interference problems. Still, these cosmic incidences should remind us just how small we really are in comparison to our Universe! And, ultimately, just how small we are in comparison to the Creator of our Universe! For any doubt that may arise in your brain (which He created too), He answers in the middle of our verse "that He is far above...or anything else." And just to be clear, He reminds us He will be above all in the future world to come as well. In thinking about the unrest in the Middle East, we may worry about what kind of leadership will become prominent and take power in these uprisings and changes in control. Even the United States is changing so quickly one cannot help but feel uncertain about our future. There is no promise our country will always be free to worship God as we are free to do today. Still, in all of this unrest, I need to have peace about who is in charge here!!! This verse reassures me I can have peace no matter who is "in charge" because we can rest in the fact our God is the greatest and there is no question for us as to who is the TOP DOG! God is above all. Period!

In thinking about our lesson yesterday and the reason we need to know our God, consider this question: How does knowing this character trait of God- that He is "above all" - make you feel in your everyday circumstances or in your particular struggles?

_____

_____

_____

Do you struggle with peace? If knowing God is "above all things" is simply not enough, think about the following passages of Scripture:

Philippians 4:6-7 (NIV)
"[6]Do not be anxious about anything, but in everything, by prayer and petition, with thanksgiving, present your requests to God. [7]And the peace of God, which transcends all understanding, will guard your hearts and your minds in Christ Jesus."

1 Peter 5:7 (NIV)
"[7]Cast all your anxiety on him because he cares for you."

Write down one action step you can take to have peace and increase your faith in God's character. Specifically, He is truly "above all things" in your life today!

_____

_____

_____

Day 5 God Over All
Read Ephesians 1:22-23

I pray the study of the first chapter of Ephesians has been a great beginning for us. Knowing who we are in Christ is so important to relating to our present pain and struggles with any sense of rationale. Just as important, if not more important, is knowing God personally and gaining the knowledge to know and understand Him more.

So as a refresher today, this is what we have learned in our quest for peace in this crazy world: Even if I question who I am, if I know who God is and He is faithful, loving, strong, true, all-powerful, and above all - with this knowledge I can make it through any day and any trial, right?

In our passage today, we learn even more about our Great God. Not only is our God above all, great and powerful, but also, He is over all!!! He is over every high place in the Heavenly. He is over all angelic beings, God is over any other position we may or may not know exists. He is the "IT" guy. Also, God the Father makes this distinct clarification He, in all His authority, has made Christ over all and even over all the church. He is the head and we are the body. He composes the brains, so to speak, and we carry out the plans. Not that God needs us by any means, but it is amazing to consider God uses us. He doesn't call us to a job and leave us to it. He equips us and makes us worthy to do a work in which even the Angels do not get to take part.

Why do you think knowing God is over all is significant to us as followers of Christ?

_____

_____

_____

In what way does understanding the position of Christ as the head of the church and we, the followers as the body of Christ make sense in the full plan and purposes of the life of the church?

_____

_____

_____

I truly understand what it means to question God's plans and purposes; but how can trusting Him help when you are questioning His plans and purposes in your life?

_____

_____

_____

In these last few verses, we conclude our second week of study. I don't know what you are dealing with this day, nor would I ever understand all of your personal struggles. Still, as a part of the body of Christ, I know when one member suffers we all suffer. In order to be an encouragement to you, I pray you know your present struggle is but for a season. We have a glorious inheritance, and you are called His inheritance. You are chosen by Him. It gave Him great pleasure to choose you! You will receive your inheritance one day. Imagine that! The very creator of the universe claims not the beautiful sands of the Gulf of Mexico, nor does He choose the snowcapped mountains of Switzerland as His inheritance, but instead He chose you and I as followers and heirs to His family. He chose us! We are his inheritance. You are special. Lavish in His love for you today. Take a hard swallow and re-boot your thinking, for you are a part of His great, mysterious plan. He wants you to know Him intimately and experience Him fully. Nothing passes through His hands that He doesn't see. He is above all and over any circumstance you may be experiencing today. You are the church. He has a plan for you, and only you, to accomplish. He is our fearless leader, and you have a future! What hope we have in Jesus!

Week Three: Baby Loss
Ephesians 2:1-22

Key Passage: We are His Masterpiece-Plans prepared
Ephesians 2:10 (NIV)

> [10]**For we are God's workmanship, created in Christ Jesus to do good works, which God prepared in advance for us to do.**

This week's key passage is Ephesians 2:10. In my story, the chapter Baby Loss tells of my experience with emotional healing. I learned one of the greatest paths for healing comes from knowing God has a master plan in mind, and He sometimes works that plan through the grief and loss of my plans and my will. This sense of God's sovereignty over my life gave me the sense that I could heal from these significant losses of little lives in my life.

As we study together, may the Spirit of the living, loving God grant to you the experience of the fullness of God's love for you, for how great is His love for you. Be diligent in your study this week, Dear One.

Day 1 You Can't Mean Me?
Read Ephesians 2:1-3

Before we fully know who we are in Christ, we need to understand who we were before Christ. This passage is a quick reminder from the Apostle Paul that we are not only an heir, a child of King Jesus, but also redeemed. There is no place for pride in our family. So often we are prone to think of ourselves more highly than we ought to, after all we are products of the self-esteem generation, right? The way I see it, as long as I know who I am in Christ and why I am in Christ, it does no harm to be reminded of who I used to be. After all, pride was the reason Satan was cast out of Heaven. Always remember, there is a thin line between pride and humility. We are all capable of the worst sin imaginable.

How can pride creep in ever so passively and puff us up?

_____

_____

_____

Do you think the Apostle knew something about humanity's tendency to swell up with pride? Surely there is a purpose for the reminder of our wretchedness before Christ in these passages of Scripture. Or perhaps the purpose in these verses is to remind us just how important it is to recognize when we knowingly do anything wrong, sinning as God calls it, we are not just serving ourselves, but serving the enemy. Verse 2 describes this walk as "obeying whom?" and why is it significant to understand?

_____

_____

_____

Even more important to understand is the fact that this way of life is assumed to be in our past. Several times the mention of the phrase "used to be" in verse 2 and the phrase "used to live that way" in verse 3 are stated. The first verse states strongly and emphatically that we were "dead" before our acceptance of Christ. Obviously, the sin in our lives before Christ did not make us physically dead, so what kind of death is implied here?

_____

_____

_____

A spiritual death is what is meant, not just for me, but for everyone that refuses God. What does the phrase in verse 3 "by our nature we were subject to God's anger" mean to you?

_____

_____

_____

In the NIV translation, the same phrase in verse 3 states, "we were deserving of God's wrath." Going back to our self-esteem generation, we may find it difficult to believe we actually "deserve" something as dreadful as "the wrath of God!"

Say it isn't so!!!

I used to ask my kindergarten students to raise their hand if they had ever done anything wrong. One year, I had a student who would NOT raise his hand. After I privately inquired about his answer, he stated: "My momma said I have NEVER done anything wrong!" Well, kudos for momma's building up a confident boy, but sad for her son never recognizing his NEED of a Savior in Jesus!!

It is not popular nor is it pleasant to evaluate our state as "dead" and "deserving the wrath of God!" Yet it is a necessary first step in the process of understanding the depths from which we came and the depths from which Jesus had to stoop to rescue us! I am not going to ask you how this makes you feel today, for any honest person must confess they have done something "wrong" in their lifetime. You see, it is our human nature to be bent on serving ourselves. At birth, the first thing an infant does is cry. The cries for need soon turn into the cries for "NOW" and so on. The progression to impatience, to demanding our wants and eventually cries of anger follow. It is hard to watch, but the cutest little two-year-old learns the word "no" much quicker than the word "yes!" Even my perfect little kindergartner had a sin problem!!! PRIDE!

Day 2 The Great But
Read Ephesians 2:4-5

Thank God for the great But! Yesterday's passages were dreadful and discouraging. I don't like to think of myself as wretched and deserving God's wrath! So today we get to tap into probably the greatest "but" in history. You see God did not leave us dead! While we were still in our sins, as we learned yesterday - dead spiritually - He died for us! I love this great exchange story. We were dead; and God sent His beloved only Son, Jesus, to rescue us and exchange our deadness for life!!! He made us alive in Jesus. This is the key and foundation for our faith. I didn't ask you to describe your feelings of spiritual deadness yesterday. Today I am more than excited to hear about your feelings of being "alive" in Christ Jesus today!!!

Describe what this means to you: "to be alive in Christ!"

_____

_____

_____

I am so thankful God didn't leave me dead in my trespasses and sin! This ol' life is so difficult the way it is, trying to simply walk with Jesus. I cannot imagine a life without Jesus as my "constant", my "go to" and my "rock!"

What specific point is the Apostle Paul making by this comparison of those who once were dead and those who have now been made alive in Christ? Just where do you think he is headed with all of this?

_____

_____

_____

First, is there a difference? Has your soul been awakened by the greatest "but" in history? Are you alive in Christ? Does His Spirit live in you as a seal/mark upon your life that HE is yours and more importantly you are HIS?

So why did God make this great exchange, an offer we can't refuse, anyway? Verse 4 answers this question.

"But because of His great _____ for us…"

Two facts emphasized in these verses are the mercy factor and the grace factor. What do you believe is the difference between mercy and grace? In these verses the writer makes sure we know it is not only while we are dead in our sins we can be made alive in Christ Jesus, but also it is because of His great love for us, His mercy, and it is totally by this little thing called "grace" that we have been saved! What is the difference between mercy and grace, and why is it important to understand their meanings?

_____

_____

_____

Grace and Mercy are two little words that are not used much in our culture. We may know girls that carry the names, but other than that we really don't use those words, unless you are playing a game where you clutch your friend's knuckles and wrestle their fingers to a submission hold! I think instead of tapping out, we are supposed to yell, mercy!!! One Bible teacher taught the difference this way:

"Grace is something we don't deserve, but God gives us anyway."

"Mercy is when we do deserve something bad…like 'the wrath of God' (Eph. 2:3), but God doesn't give it to us!!"

Thank you, Lord, for being a loving, gracious, and merciful God!!!

Day 3 Raising up an Ol' Dead Soul
Read Ephesians 2:6 - 9

Amazingly, skimming over Scripture without really chewing on it is like a cow chewing its cud. It is a bad habit we all get into at times. I was born and raised in Indiana so seeing a cow chew and digest his cud resonates with me visually. What I mean is we need to digest the meaning and consider with much thought what the Spirit of God is saying. It is as if we know it all and have heard it all before, but often times we are simply lazy or passive. When I stop and take the time to read and re-read over a passage of Scripture, the meaning and significance pops out at me fresh and new. Things I had never thought about rush through me. I am sure this is what it means by the Scripture being "alive" in us. (Hebrews 4:12) We can read and re-read history, science, and especially math (my least favorite subject), but nothing printed will pierce our hearts or make us want to move forward morally except reading the Scriptures combined with the power that is in the Spirit of God. This is what guides us into all truth (John 16:13). We find that we want to make adjustments in our lives! When we take the time to think or meditate, the messages of the truth of the Bible move us to action. That is a part of what being alive in Christ is all about. Who would want any part of a dead faith? Not I! With all of this deadness, verse 6 points out an interesting few tidbits to chew upon today.

What do you think they are?

_____

_____

_____

Did you catch all of that?

There was more than one being raised up on Resurrection Day!!! We were right there being raised up with Jesus! When Jesus went to the cross, He took all of our sins upon Himself and paid for them all. All of humanity's past, present, and future was paid for. When He died that day all sin died with Him. All of our sins went to the grave with Him. According to the passage in Ephesians, all of our deadness went with Him. When He arose from the dead after three days He raised us up along with Him. Not only did he raise us up out of our deadness, He seated us with Him in the Heavenly realms in Christ Jesus! Now that is kind of a tough cud to chew upon.

Digest that one a moment and describe what you believe this means?

Continuing on with our study of verse 6, I am going to have to pause here for a while as we research this thing out, because this is some heavy theology! I mean, I know walking on this Earth is definitely not my idea of being seated in a Heavenly Realm. And if it is supposed to be, then something has got to give here. I want hope for Heaven, not hope for what I am experiencing now! I don't want Heaven to be more of the same, thank you! So just what does this mean?

I don't know if I am even smart enough to comment on this idea. But here it goes…heavenly places means… heavenly places. If we are truly in Him and He is in us, we go where He goes and He goes where we go. I don't quite understand it, especially the idea that I am in Him also. I understand vaguely the idea that HE is in me through the indwelling of the Spirit. However, the opposite idea of me in Him is baffling. So be baffled today. Yes, it is ok to not fully understand everything.

Now, on to grace. There is one thing I am absolutely, positively, undeniably certain about and that is Ephesians 2:8-9.

This is one of the most studied Scriptures in my life. I cannot pinpoint why, other than the fact my Bible teachers wanted to drill down the idea I had nothing to do with saving myself. The simple fact is that Jesus had everything to do with saving me, not anything I do or could do. Let me reiterate again: it was through, by, and only through Jesus that I am saved.

Did I say Jesus alone?

I am reminded of the Tidy Bowl commercials that have aired on TV since I was a little girl… the bubbles would swirl around and around the toilet bowl shouting, "We work hard so you don't have tooooooo!" This is what Jesus did. He cleaned up our mess in the bowl! This pride sin rears up its ugly head so much that these verses are pounded and pounded into our heads and hearts until we are blue in the face! Jesus did it, not me! Not you! Not anything you could do or would ever want to do. I wouldn't want to do anything like go to a cross and die… so thank you, Jesus. At the risk of sounding obnoxiously insane by overstating this fact and at the risk of some thinking that I am sacrilegious, I pray you understand the significance of this fact. I have come to see my teacher's point of view. There are so many other faiths in our world where one must do something to earn grace, or somehow work hard enough to become a recipient of mercy, people miss the simple truth that, yes, Jesus loves me so much He did it all for me so I don't have tooooooo!!!!

What are your thoughts about "doing" verses "receiving" grace from God…Working your way to God compared to receiving grace from God.

_____

_____

_____

I know in the midst of turmoil and difficulties I need to have rock solid truths I believe about my faith. This is definitely one of those rock solid foundational truths! Jesus loves me this much that He did it ALL so I don't have to!

What about you? How does the fact that Jesus did it all for you help you in times of struggles and trials in your life?

_____

_____

_____

_____

_____

_____

Day 4 A Life Coach
Read Ephesians 2:10-18

So much to consider today, but the meat of the matter is God has a plan for us! If God Himself were on the Social Media, He could be our "Life Coach." He has all the answers, and He is available to help coach us through life. Best of all, He is FREE! Since He is our "Life Coach," it is prudent to understand what He thinks is best for our lives. The Apostle Paul is trying to get these early followers to grasp their game! He urges them to see that they are big players in this master plan of God's. In God's game they are more than players, and the focus is on them and their role in this plan as the "masterpiece" that God is always working on. (vs.10) This masterpiece is called you and me. We are the Michael Jordans in this plan - the star players. We have been designed for specific purposes. These plans have been ongoing for a long time according to this verse. How long has God had your purpose and plan in mind?

_____

_____

_____

How does this make you feel even in the middle of the junk you may be enduring or have gone through in your life?

_____

_____

_____

With the consideration of the culture in which the Apostle Paul was writing, how huge was the impact God had made a way for the Gentile people to become followers of Christ as well as the chosen Jews?

_____

_____

_____

How might we carry this idea of unity and peace into our current culture?

_____

_____

_____

Can you see the relevance of this idea of peace and Jesus as our peacemaker carried out even in our local bodies of believers today? How can we build unity in our local churches since this idea is so important?

_____

_____

_____

Verse 14 is one of my favorite verses in this study because the simple fact Jesus is our peace. Nothing more and nothing less is needed. What He did on the cross has broken down any and all walls of hostility between the Jewish people and the Gentile people of that time and also any hostility that would divide us today.

He is our peace. He has broken down every wall of hostility, division, among us. He desires unity. It must start inward and overflow to others. Peace with God and peace with self. Peace with others- those in our home first, then peace and unity in our body of believers. With this kind of incredible peace those not yet in Christ will truly see the love of God or, better yet, they will be attracted to this unique love. Recently I've been wrestling with excuses of why I can't have peace, unity, and love in my home. I don't know about your home, but at times mine seems like World War 3!!!

And yet I have found the level of peace boils down to my level of faith about God as my peace. Either He has broken down every wall- even those walls that seem insurmountable - or He has not. If He has not, I must conclude He does not do what He says He has done. I wonder if when I question Him and those outside of my family and in my community notice, do I cause others to question? Does my lack of peace cause those who do not believe yet to question faith in Jesus because of my lack of belief, lack of unity, lack of love and lack of peace?

I know the area of peace, where I need Jesus to be in the dead center, is in my home. With sibling rivalry, frustrations that accompany a special needs child, and every other battle that weighs against my family on a daily basis, I need Jesus to go to the wall and break it down as only He is able and He is capable. This unity principle is so vitally important, because without peace you will not have unity! Look at what the book of John has to say about unity!

> "[20]My prayer is not for them alone. I pray also for those who will believe in me through their message, [21]that all of them may be one, Father, just as you are in me and I am in you. May they also be in us so that the world may believe that you have sent me. [22]I have given them the glory that you gave me, that they may be one as we are one: [23]I in them and you in me. May they be brought to complete unity to let the world know that you sent me and have loved them even as you have loved me." (John 17:20-23)

The Scripture speaks about the significance of the followers of Jesus having unity. How does this message impact your family? This is vitally important to grasp even in our own struggles. Why do you agree or disagree?

_____

_____

_____

Yep, this is all wrapped up in God's ultimate plan and purpose for my life as an individual. He is working out his masterpiece in and through you and me. I believe it starts in our hearts, moves through our homes, then trickles out through our communities. When a lost and hopeless person sees the love and unity we have for each other, especially in our homes, then they see the peace that only comes through Jesus. This is what John 17 is teaching us. This great love for each other is what is so attractive to those not yet in Christ.

Day 5 A Master Plan
Read Ephesians 2:19-22

God's Master plan and purpose for me as an individual, wrapped up yesterday's key emphasis. I pray the study left you with the grounded belief that whatever you are going through today is never out of control, nor did it just slip through God's hand. He has allowed it for the over-arching purposes of fulfilling His Master plan. This is the plan He has for you and me, founded and created from long ago. We matter and what we suffer through matters. He loves us this much and I don't want you to ever forget it! Still, even more than our individual purposes and plans, God has a master plan for all believers from all times and to all ages. What is the desire for the entirety of believers as found in Ephesians 2:21?

_____

_____

_____

Yes, we are called a Holy Temple, where God dwells and we dwell among all people, nations, and races. We are in Christ Jesus, and there is no wall of division among us all. Have you ever been around "those" people just beam with love and ooze niceties? They just smile about everything and have something positive to say about everyone. They even turn your most horrific experiences into something you can accept as a gift from God! I am not one of "those" people, yet. I don't know if I ever will be a person who oozes niceties here on this earth, but I do love being around "those" people. They are almost always encouragers, interested in my needs. They rarely mention anything at all about their life, although I am sure they have needs too! This is the type of "attraction" that love and unity brings to a group of people. This is the type of selfless attitude of always putting others' needs above their own needs that is only ascertained through following the model of Jesus. When we seek to be like Jesus, this attraction becomes more and more apparent. People are drawn to it. The Scripture calls it holiness or sanctification. And don't get me wrong, there is a process of ridding oneself of self and sin and any other thing that would not reflect Christ, but this attraction is so appealing to people. Another way to look at it is like this… these people so ooze Jesus that people want what they have. They may not even mention the name of Jesus at first, but their love for others so overflows that people want to be around them and seek to gain what they are experiencing. The great news is this is our Holy Calling as a church and we can be "those" kind of people. So, what level of ooziness are you? Are you willing to be what it takes to attract those not yet in Christ? More importantly, in your sphere of influence who are you praying and seeking to attract to Jesus?

Jew or Gentile. If you are in Christ you are a part of this family. You are a royal citizen. This is your Holy Calling. I know it is a huge responsibility...and most of the time I just want to hide away from people, because my neighbors certainly must hear the chaos that echoes through my walls into their homes. Most of the time I simply try to keep a long distance from my neighbors because I know the down and dirty of the daily grind in my household! Not very spiritual, I know, but the truth of the matter is it is downright difficult to be "those" kind of people. I don't think much of what I have to offer is very "attractive," not even close. Most of the time I think we are just "repulsive" for Christ!!! Maybe that is why I write - because you don't have to live near my family and me! I do say this in jest (mostly), but it can be difficult. The trials and troubles we face on a daily basis make it tough to be the Holy Church Christ so desires, don't they?

I am not going to give up though. I am sure glad that that phrase says in verse 21 "becoming a holy temple for the Lord," instead of the emphasis on "we have arrived!"

In spite of myself, I am going to press on and try to place more energy and time into those closest to me. One day the struggles will end. There will be a day when all that has been promised will come to pass, and we will not grieve as we do in this life. We will not worry over divisions, but peace will prevail and love will win! This is part of those blessings we worked so hard to grasp in the beginning of this great study. Hold tight to the truth. Sometimes that is all we have to cling to!

I pray you have grasped the foundational truth this week that God has a plan for the church and it includes you! Every little detail matters in our lives; every joy and every hurt matter to Him. It would be much easier to get bitter about the losses in life, but quite frankly, I have tried that path and it really doesn't offer much. It is definitely not very attractive and honestly, not many people want to be around bitterness. But a road to "becoming?" Now that is a road worth traveling. He sees you on your journey and you are His Masterpiece!

Week Four: Sugar & Spice
Ephesians 3:1-21

Key Passage – Understanding How Much He Loves Us
Ephesians 3:16-19 (NIV)

> **"[16]I pray that out of his glorious riches he may strengthen you with power through his Spirit in your inner being, [17]so that Christ may dwell in your hearts through faith. And I pray that you, being rooted and established in love, [18]may have power, together with all the saints, to grasp how wide and long and high and deep is the love of Christ, [19]and to know this love that surpasses knowledge--that you may be filled to the measure of all the fullness of God."**

My story of loss and confusion over the main question of why God would give me a child with the mental difficulties and disabilities, an adult daughter that struggles to overcome these difficulties daily, is rooted in the study of this week's key passages of Scripture. Wrestling down just how much God really loves me has made living with the daily loss of a special needs child, now adult, bearable for me. I pray whatever your story today, that God's love will make what you are going through bearable and even full of joy! Whether in loss or in gain, may you hold on to this promise of His great love for you, friend.

As we study together, may the Spirit of the living, loving God grant to you the experience of the fullness of God's love for you, for I pray you know now just how much He loves you!

Day 1 Credentials
Read Ephesians 3:1-8

Again, we see the Apostle Paul explaining his responsibility to make known to the Jewish community of believers and to the Gentile community of believers that it is God's perfect plan for all to come to faith in Jesus Christ. One of the most quoted and taught verses in the entire Bible in our modern society is John 3:16. This verse emphasizes the same thought in our passages of study today: "whosoever," (anyone Jew or Gentile) should have the gift of eternal life in Christ Jesus. One thought I found interesting while studying this passage of Scripture was the fact that the Old Testament prophesies foretold the Gentiles would one day turn to God and be saved. However, the organic unity and equality that happened between the believing Jews and the Gentiles was highly unexpected.

Let's read through this Old Testament prophecy that has come to pass in Romans 15:9-12.

"^{9}so that the Gentiles may glorify God for his mercy, as it is written: "Therefore I will praise you among the Gentiles; I will sing hymns to your name." ^{10}Again, it says, "Rejoice, O Gentiles, with his people." ^{11}And again, "Praise the Lord, all you Gentiles, and sing praises to him, all you peoples." ^{12}And again, Isaiah says, "The Root of Jesse will spring up, one who will arise to rule over the nations; the Gentiles will hope in him."(Romans 15:9-12)

As we consider our lives and the daily grind many of us endure, what relevance does knowing and understanding the fulfillment of prophecy have to do with anything in your life today?

Write your thoughts:

_____

_____

_____

As we recall the solid foundation of the first chapter of Ephesians and the premise of knowing who we are in Christ Jesus, it is just as vitally important to grasp again and again, as we walk through trials in this life, that we know who Christ Jesus is. Prophecies are the messages spoken by spiritual leaders to the people many years before they were to come to pass. They are sort of like predictions of what is going to occur. So, the fulfillment of prophecies gives us solid rocks we can build our faith upon. These are truths that confirm and affirm God is who He says He is and that Jesus is indeed who He says He is. The idea a Jew and Gentile would be unified in any matter was just a ridiculous, if not seemingly impossible notion for that culture. I am sure those Psalmists took a lot of slack for singing those songs. The crowd may have even thrown tomatoes at them. To compare the absurdity of the notion to today, it would be like the Palestine state joining in unity with the country of Israel. So now the more we digest and chew on this idea, not much has changed in several hundred years. It is clear why the Apostle Paul keeps reiterating the message. It is clear why it was kept a mystery and now it is even clearer why the Apostle keeps trying to persuade his readers with his credentials.

As I grow in my walk with Jesus, I am learning I question Him more and carry more doubt when things are going badly in my life. The doubt seems to creep in when life sucks the wind out of me. In those tough times, I simply question. I question the validity of the truths I so passionately write about today. Honestly, how do you respond in tough times? Do you ever question if this whole Bible thing is a story or if God is really who He says He is?

I know it is okay to question. I think if we are not honest about our questions first, and try to work out our questions to resolutions, then sometimes we blindly follow what someone else believes. That is not faith or an authentic relationship with Christ; it is simple ignorance. In raising a special needs child, the conflict that arises from her non-compliance can be overwhelming a lot of the time. The crazy thing is the same issues arise. She usually does not want to do what I ask her to do. Just like a typical teenager. Then again, she likes to help a lot of the time as well, so it really depends on her mood. Well, as many of you know, depending upon an adolescent's mood is risky business!!!! Still, with her disabilities, she doesn't act or react the same way a typical teenager would act. Instead of talking back and rolling her eyes, she throws a two-year-old, yelling, screaming, "I want my way," fit. The main problem with this is she is now 175 pounds of solid person! So, trying to be a consistent parent, and not give into her every whim and need, is a difficult choice because I know what the outcome will be if she decides to be non-compliant! I doubt many can relate to the issues of raising a special child, but I am confident you have your own set of issues in your life. So, what do you do with your daily grind? When life throws you a curveball? You have to know what you believe for you! I have found the closer I lean into Jesus, ask questions, study, take steps of faith and see God come through time and time again, my faith grows stronger and I have less questions and doubt and more perseverance to walk through the junk!

What about you? What makes or breaks your faith?

How do you work through your questions?

_____

_____

_____

Unfortunately, perseverance stinks! I would rather experience instant sanctification than endure another dose of the "same" every day. Still, it is the thing that moves us closer to who God wants us to be in this world. It is His process to becoming more like Jesus, however difficult.

I wonder if in verse 1 of our study today, when the Apostle Paul explains all of his current struggles and trials were for the Gentiles' benefit, if the message isn't the same for us today. Sometimes I believe God uses our struggles and trials for the benefit of others, those outside of Christ, just like the Gentiles of decades past, for the benefit of their coming to faith in Jesus. Take heart today, whatever you are going through; God can use it for the benefit of someone else. Let's not waste our hurts but encourage others through our hurts today.

Day 2 A Colorful Variety
Read Ephesians 3:9-12

The mystery the Apostle Paul is revealing gets even more mysterious to me as we consider these verses today.

Why does the wisdom of God come in a variety to those unseen authorities and rulers?

What does that mean? I think we can consider the world before the sacrifice of Jesus as cold, stale, and dead. Think of this age as somewhat like an old black and white movie. Remember the movie, "Schindler's List?"[1] The entire film was created intentionally in black and white. When, at the end of the movie, the little girl was dressed in a "red" coat, the essence of the story came together brilliantly in that one moment in time. I remember that moment in the film; it is hopelessly etched in my memories forever. I believe the entire universe was like that black and white movie until the cross, when in that moment in time Christ spilled His love upon the cross for all of us. Yet, unlike Schindler's List, I believe the church has colorful moments we as individuals and as groups of believers accomplish and the God of the Universe sketches in the minds of those not yet in Christ. They see the color and pause. Many pause, consider, and move on with their lives. Others pause, consider, and move a step closer to Jesus. For some that colorful moment in time may be the moment when they place their faith and trust in Jesus.

The verses express this wisdom as unique wisdom that comes through the church. By observing the church, the principalities and invisible spiritual kingdom are learning this unique wisdom. Why would God want this unseen kingdom/spiritual kingdom, made up of good and evil, to see this wisdom? The revelation is the love of God in ways the angels cannot experience themselves because they know only God's holiness. Why then? I submit to you when God's love is demonstrated to the lost through the church, the angels are amazed, and the dark, demonic world is once again reminded they are already defeated. God's love is always an expression of color. Because of the cross, Blue Mondays turn suddenly into golden moments of glory! Dark hours of discouragement are now lifted to bright visions of our hope in Christ. In all of these moments in our lives, because of the cross the dull, cold times in life are changed to colorful moments, when the body of Christ - the church - learns to trust God and lose our fears. In the hour of pressure and discouragement, as we lean into our Lord, we make God's love made known to all! Not just those in our sphere of influence here on earth, but the Bible also tells us the angels give glory to God when they see us trusting God through his love.

If these colorful, God-ordained moments are translated as a display of the rich variety of the wisdom of God at work, then this is our story! What is a colorful moment in your life? Describe a colorful moment that you can absolutely identify as part of the work of God through you? Or consider what you could share with the group that you know is only the result of God's colorful riches of wisdom in your life?

_____

_____

_____

Each story is evidence of the riches that come from this mystery that is now what we call the Gospel of Jesus Christ.

All that is right and good in our culture is a result of the Light that has come into our dark world. Jesus is the Light of the World. How often do we think about all we have because of Jesus? Write down a few things in which you can see God's light in our dark world shining through.

_____

_____

_____

Isaiah 9:1-7 is the prophecy of the coming of Jesus as the Light in the darkness.
Please take time to read Isaiah 9:1-7. Here the Light in the darkness is revealed as THE light.

Because there is so much in these particular verses, I want to focus on the great message found in verse 12. Because of God's great love for us, we have more than just a shoulder to lean on in Jesus; we have access to come to Christ personally. Before the cross the Jewish people could only access God through the high priest who would enter the Holy of Holies in the Temple on their behalf. At the cross, the prophecy of Matthew 27:51 was fulfilled when the curtain inside the Holy of Holies was torn in two. We were and are now granted access to come before our God in a personal way. No longer do we rely upon another; no longer would we have a long distance relationship with God. We now have 24/7 access to our Father. Anytime, anyplace, we can call upon Him and He will hear us and answer us.

Through the colorful moments of life, how does it make you feel knowing you have a 24/7 God who hears and answers you?

_____

_____

_____

Day 3 Paul's Prayer Part One
Read Ephesians 3:13-17

This is one of my favorite passages of the Bible. I suppose this is because it gives me so much hope, and I see it as a responsibility for me as a leader to pray like Paul for those God has entrusted me to lead.

The first part of Paul's prayer at a glance may seem like the Apostle is trying to encourage the believers he is okay and for them not to worry about him even though at the present time he is being held in Rome on house arrest. As we consider the culture and time in which these early believers lived, we will realize the Apostle Paul is not trying to alleviate the believers' worry for him as much as he is trying to alleviate their worry for their own skins! These believers were not any different from us. Just like us, they didn't want to go through persecution, trials, and distress! We cannot even come close to comprehending the terror and unrest these early believers were facing.

If we had any clue as to what kind of persecution these people endured, we too would fall on our faces before God and pray for strength! The Apostle knew they would need not just physical strength, but a strength that comes from way down deep inside, in the core of their being. For these early believers to persevere, endure, and continue in the faith, they would need a deeper faith then they currently held. What resource would this strength come from, and how would they receive it?

_____

_____

_____

The ultimate powerhouse is found in God - the Creator of the Universe, the Glorious God whose resources are limitless! I don't know about you, but I'm a little more courageous today just reading about the accessible power force that is available to you and me. When you consider the trials or battles you may endure today, how does meditating and considering our Great and Powerful God make you feel?

_____

_____

_____

Now that we know our power source and that through the Spirit He gives us inner strength, "how" do we gain or "plug into" this source for our daily living? It is one thing to think about or ponder the greatness of God, but if I never "plug into" or tap the power source, my circuit remains open, and basically the lights are still off!!! You've heard the old saying, "the lights are on but nobody's home!" Have you ever experienced a situation where you were home, scared, full of failures, and apprehensive about the future? It seemed your lights were off, and the lights are OFF! One thing that adds fear to any circumstance or situation is to be alone in the dark! In the dark, our own imaginations creep us out. I took my son to a scare house once. He had been begging us to take him for years. We finally gave in, and I was the "lucky one" chosen to take him and his friend. The funny thing was we arrived so early all of the creepy "scare" tactics started before the sun actually went down. We saw them in the light of day. When the sun did set and darkness fell, it really was amusing because our minds remembered what the creeps looked like and what they did in the daylight, thus making them a lot less creepy and a lot less scary at night.

All that to say, we don't have to live in the dark, we have the ultimate power source at our very fingertips.

Verse 17 states, "as we trust in Christ, then, He makes His home in your hearts." (NLT) I have wondered so many times why pastors and evangelists tell people to ask Jesus into their hearts. This is so cool to understand that for one, the Bible says in James 2:19 "You believe that there is one God. Good! Even the demons believe that - and shudder" So we know that there is more to just having a "belief" in God or that Jesus is God, or even knowing Jesus died on the cross. Even the demons know that! So there is definitely more to be said about Christ making His home in your hearts. The previous verse answers how God makes this transformation happen and says this inner strength, trust, and home-making come through whom?

_____

_____

_____

As we learned earlier in Ephesians 1:13 & 14 the Spirit is our seal and guarantee of our redemption. The Spirit is our hope of inheritance, and He is also the one who is "deposited" into our hearts. Once this deposit takes place He dwells in our hearts. What does it mean for the Spirit to dwell in your heart?

_____

_____

_____

I know I just had you answer a very deep theological question about your faith. Yet this one question, whether Christ dwells in your heart or He does not, is the most significant question of all mankind. It is the question all humankind asks: Am I in or am I not?"

Still, in verse 17, the presence of the Spirit in your heart is not just the goal. It is like our inviting a neighbor to visit our homes, and as they enter our foyer, we simply go about our daily routine of cleaning, sweeping the floors, washing the dishes, reading our mail, without conversation, interaction, or even acknowledgment of their presence in our homes. Yes, we invited them into our homes - they are present - but this passage begs the question of cultivation. Using agricultural terms, the Apostle admonishes us to action as well. We do not simply "Plug into" the power source, but we also need to cultivate our lives to grow "strong" roots driven into His love. Just as we make our homes warm and inviting for those we entertain, we need to make our hearts a home for God the Spirit. How often do I cultivate my relationship with God the Spirit, or even acknowledge His presence in my heart, His home? And what are some ways I can be a warm, inviting home for His presence in my heart?

_____

_____

_____

As we develop into the person in whom the Spirit wants to dwell, we become stronger and our power source is more lit than dark, thus empowering us to do the works He has planned for us to do.

Day 4 Paul's Prayer Part Two
Ephesians 3:18-19

We talked yesterday about our great power source, which we have available to meet our every issue, need or even crisis. We also discussed how we grow stronger through cultivating the presence of the Spirit living within our hearts. We discover today the understanding of just how much He loves us.

Through the doubt of loss and pain I have realized this very thing: I know "HE LOVES ME THIS MUCH"

Simply, If I know how much God loves me then I can get through anything this life throws at me! I say this cautiously, because I have not been through all that life can throw at a person. And I don't really want to experience all! Nor do you! But I know the grief of the daily losses that disappoint and discourage me are just temporary. When I deeply consider (not just think in passing) about His love, but truly know the depth, the height, the breadth, the length of His love for me, the Scriptures teach a "completeness" that accompanies this full understanding. Yet the apostle is quick to remark, as am I, we cannot fully understand God's love. His great love is too great to fully understand! Why do you think we cannot fully understand His love?

_____

_____

_____

As you experience His great love for you, what is it about His love that gives you a state of completeness?

_____

_____

_____

In the following spaces write after each phrase your own statement for what that kind of love means to you

God's love is wide

_____

_____

_____

God's love is long.

_____

_____

_____

God's love is high.

_____

_____

_____

God's love is deep.

_____

_____

_____

Whatever His love has grown to mean to you, cling to it. And, as you grow in Him and He in you, as your faith journey unfolds before your path, no matter what you go through today or what you may go through tomorrow, may His love always be constant in your heart and mind.

Day 5 More Than You Can Ever Imagine
Read Ephesians 3:20-21

As I begin this devotional day, I am enjoying listening to worship music. One particular song is playing that reminds me of what God has planned for my future, my family's future, and for this passage as it directly applies to my life. Being a church plant in the middle of a large city comes with great responsibility. There is song whose lyrics claim, "greater things are still to come… greater things are yet to be done in this city."[2] As the lyrics repeat over and over I want to jump out of my skin with anticipation for what these "greater" things are going to be. I tell you, I can't wait sometimes! God has been so faithful to my husband and me. I believe God has allowed us to witness miracle after miracle so much so I am sure I have missed some of them. Still, every time I hear that particular song, it truly is a reminder, an encouragement, and an inspiration to my heart. I do not think it was coincidence that that very worship song came on my Pandora radio right as I was about to pen thoughts on "more than you can ever imagine." Whatever you are thinking about and dreaming for God to accomplish in you and through you in your life, if God is in it, nothing can stand against your dream. "If God is for us, who can be against us?" (Romans 8:31) If you are truly pure in your motivation, then verse 20 of our Ephesians passage expresses you should just go ahead and count it as done. Whatever great work you're considering, because HE will accomplish infinitely more!! Not just what we are thinking about - no, my friend, it will be more! Not just more than we are dreaming for Him to accomplish through us, it will be infinitely more! I can assure you, the truth is not a lie. When we started praying about a church that would target a generation that was drifting farther and farther away from the faith, we had no idea three couples in the living room of our little suburban home would see God grow us from 6 to 40, and from 140 to 440, and from 440 to 640, and still growing. So many people told us twenty-year-olds would not be able to financially pay for a church. We moved into our building with zero debt, because God raised the $260,000 to pay off renovations in the middle of the worst recession of our times! Today over six years later we have miraculously purchased our building. If you think God has not accomplished infinitely more than we could ever hope, dream or imagine I would dare to differ with you.

What are you dreaming for the Kingdom of God? Is there something that keeps you up at night? Not just your job, bills, family woes, but what is that thing that is not "right" in the world that God keeps tugging at your heart?

_____

_____

_____

I have experienced so much of the "more" in these verses, and the truth does not state that I should expect a limit upon the "more." What does the verse say about the amount or measure to which we can expect God to accomplish His mighty, powerful work in us?

_____

_____

_____

While the NLT expresses the word as infinitely, other versions of the Bible state "beyond" and simply "more." Read the Amplified Version for verse 20 to fully digest the impact of what the Apostle Paul is trying to convey.

"Now to Him Who, by (in consequence of) the (action of His) power that is at work within us, is able to (carry out His purpose and) do superabundantly, far over and above all that we (dare) ask or think (infinitely beyond our highest prayers, desires, thoughts, hopes, or dreams)" (Ephesians 3:20 AMB)

Another song came to mind as I was scripting this verse into our study, not quite as spiritual as the first song, yet appropriate and whimsical. This time the singer is Mary Poppins!

"Supercalifragilisticexpialidocious!

Even though the sound of it is something quite atrocious…"[3]

Well, maybe the sound of this expectation God has given us so freely and attainably sounds… precocious as well. Maybe you think we do not deserve to see God move on our behalf in such a supercalifragilisticexpialidocious manner? If you are feeling precocious about the thought, take a gander at verse 21. This verse puts it all into perspective.

What does verse 21 teach us about the experiences God gives us in verse 20?

_____

_____

_____

I am certain that "all" praise and glory for anything God chooses to accomplish in us and through us is for God's praise. Still, I hope you did not miss one other key thought in the verse. The words "throughout all generations" have a significant meaning as well; I do not know about you, but I want my kids to experience all God has and wants to accomplish through them also. I believe as they grow up and see God working such miraculous wonders and the infinitely more in my life, they will be challenged and have the hunger to experience God's infinitely more for their lives. This is the generational praise and glory is due our great and awesome God.

What are your thoughts about this generational praise?

_____

_____

_____

Week Five: Love Loss
Ephesians 4:1-32

Key Passage: Making allowances because of your love
Ephesians 4:1-2 (NIV)

> "**[1]As a prisoner for the Lord, then, I urge you to live a life worthy of the calling you have received. [2]Be completely humble and gentle; be patient, bearing with one another in love.**"

This week's key passages are from Ephesians is 4:1-2. Every time I share the love loss of my life, I feel a bit of remorse. While my story will definitely resonate with so many people who have gone through betrayal in their relationship, I still hate the fact it exposes my husband's character flaw. He is truly an awesome man of God; and God has used our past to help so many people in their present. The importance of making allowances for the faults of our loved ones is a message that must be shared and received. For this reason, I continue to share my love loss. Because of our love for each other and our love for the Lord, we share openly and willingly the message of forgiveness and restoration. Our prayer is you will be able to make allowances in your love relationships "because of your love." Whether you need this message today in your own relationship or not, may you use this message of forgiveness as a gift to those that need it. Our marriages are supposed to be the primary picture that reflects Christ's love to the church - His bride. Additionally, our study this week speaks to our hearts on the subject of unity. In order to have unity in our homes and churches we have to practice making allowances.

As we study together, may the Spirit of the living, loving God grant to you the experience of the fullness of God's love for you, because He truly loves you so much! Be studious in your study, my friend.

Day 1 Hey You
Read Ephesians 4:1-12

As we briefly touched on in the earlier chapters of Ephesians, God has already prepared specific and unique abilities and plans for us to accomplish. This first verse emphasizes doubly the point that each person is truly called by God to a specific work for the Kingdom. We are to make ourselves worthy of this calling, and we must realize we have a particular calling. No, not everyone will be a teacher or preacher, but we all must be a "reacher" for Christ. Whatever you discover your specific calling is, I guarantee God has in mind someone who will be "reached" by Christ through you and your work. These works are definitely Kingdom business. Thus, we are to be worthy of the Kingdom business. It is interesting to me that directly after we are admonished to be worthy of our calling, we are directed to some ways we are to act on our journey to being worthy. List below the four key components of verse 2 with regard to how we are to be worthy of our calling?

1. _____

2. _____

3. _____

4. _____

These four actions (humble, gentle, patient, and forgiving) are tied up with a bow at the end of the verses in 3 and 4 with an emphasis on unity. Unity is obviously a goal in our relationships and is emphatically expressed throughout Ephesians. Here we see it emphasized again.

I have to admit being proud, harsh, impatient, and even holding unattainable expectations is how I too often describe my responses. Unfortunately, my children get to feel the full brunt of these opposite and unworthy reactions! Why is it my unworthiness of my calling always seems to be exposed in my reactions and attitudes toward those I love the most? Can you relate?

I believe for this reason God placed these four key components right after His plea to live a life worthy of our calling. God knows we struggle and treat those closest to us the worst. He knows if we can have true unity - starting with humility, gentleness, patience and, yes, preparing ourselves for the likelihood we will need to exercise and extend forgiveness to our family members on a daily basis (with our families first and foremost), then we will be more likely to treat others rightly. And by others I mean our neighbors, co-workers, friends and acquaintances. My husband makes this statement often: "the light that shines the farthest, shines the brightest at home." With this statement in mind, why do you believe God wraps our worthiness of our calling into our daily attitudes including the way we treat those in our immediate families?

_____

_____

_____

Sometimes it just seems easier to expect less of strangers and treat those you do not know very well with the highest level of grace, humility, gentleness, patience, and even forgiveness. We even let things go so much easier outsiders offend us. Still, our true character shines the brightest when no one else is looking. If we can exercise extended amounts of grace and forgiveness doused with doses of gentleness and humility within the four walls of our homes, then I think we are less likely to be a liability for the name of Christ and, thus, be worthy of our calling.

Stop now and consider your relationships. Is there anyone in your life you need to "make an allowance for?"

The following passages talk about several gifts that are given to the church. The gifts are: apostles, prophets, evangelist, pastors, and teachers.
Rather than key in on each of these specific gifts, let's think about the following verse. Verse 12 states the responsibilities these gifted people are to exercise for the church as a whole. What are the two responsibilities?

_____

_____

_____

As we consider the admonishment given to each and every believer in Ephesians, we are also given works to be done. We are given a specific calling and we are to live worthy of this great calling of God. Our church leaders are responsible **to equip us and build us up** in our specific callings. How does the reality you have such a specific calling, and God's plan is you develop this calling make you feel?

_____

_____

_____

Have you narrowed down what you believe is your calling? Or is this is a new discovery for you? Do you have any inclination of what you believe your calling might be? Don't worry or be anxious…this does not have to be determined today.

_____

_____

_____

Take time today to pray and ask the Lord to reveal your calling. If you are certain what God's calling is for you, pray He will give you a fresh zeal to accomplish the works He has prepared for you.

Day 2 What Is My Calling?
Read Ephesians 4:7-13

Do not feel bad if you were unable to pinpoint your specific calling. Many believers often go through life thinking they are not called vocationally, thinking they are simply supposed to attend church and do a few service projects, maybe even join a Bible Study or two, and possibly even share their faith story with a neighbor. Simply stated, that is what many believe God expects of them. While all of that is great and God does want us to do all of those great things, sometimes we totally miss our callings in the middle of these great, religious activities in which we participate.

Have you ever felt you were participating in "religious activities?" Why do you think you feel that way?

_____

_____

_____

I pray this study has been enlightening in this truth we are all called! I know not all of us will be called to be an apostle, a prophet, an evangelist, a pastor or even a teacher; still we each need to take the responsibility for those works that are alluded to in Ephesians 1. The great news is God does not hide these works from us; and quite frankly, you may already be doing exactly the works God has called you to do

A great practice when contemplating our giftedness is to consider what it is that keeps you up at night. Is there anything that consumes you? In modernity, this idea is often called a "holy discontent." What is it that you see as just "wrong" in our world? It could also be some event that makes you feel satisfied when you participate in it. Or possibly your "holy discontent" occurs when you want to rise up and "do" something about an injustice?

Asking yourself these probing questions can help you navigate the works God has called you to accomplish for the Kingdom. In I Corinthians, we are given a list of the typical "gifts" that are called the spiritual gifts. These are commonly taught as the gifts God distributes as He sees fit to all believers. While each believer is uniquely wired, created, and given gifts, the works I am referring to are more "theme" oriented and idea driven. These works are birthed in the believer. While a believer may have the gift of serving, I believe they can serve in multiple areas of a church or body of believers. Another example would be a believer given the gift of hospitality - while this believer may love entertaining within their home, and they may even host a home Bible study, I believe that they bring to the Kingdom specific works that they are called to accomplish for God. I think God births a specific calling or "work" that only that believer can accomplish for the Kingdom of God, and I believe God has prepared these works for that particular believer before that person was even conceived. How do you feel about this knowledge? Does the weight of this responsibility change the way you previously thought about your gifting and calling? If so, How?

_____

_____

_____

Forgiveness is emphasized in our key passages yesterday, but I am not saying that forgiving my husband for his betrayal was easy. It was not. It was one of the greatest hurts of my life, and it was only the example of Christ's extension of love and forgiveness of my sins that gave me the grace to extend forgiveness to him. It was because of our love we were able to forgive. Verse 13 talks about being mature in the Lord. Only through unity can we try to attain this maturity. Yet, authentic unity can only come through a heart that is full of forgiveness. Since this is only accomplished when we are willing to forgive, I must submit to you this question again: If you have someone you need to forgive, won't you extend forgiveness today? If not for your own emotional healing, but for love, God's love, because HE FORGAVE you. Will you forgive?

Day 3 Be Steady, Be Ready
Read Ephesians 4:14-16

Are you the kind of person that is more inclined to be skeptical, or are you more inclined to be naïve?

I have found I seem to question teaching more than I just accept it. Does that make me a bad person? I mean, how could I question the teaching of a Godly leader who has spent hours in preparation and study to give a message? I know most leaders would never try to mislead or misrepresent the truth of the Bible, and most understand the position of leadership (especially teaching and pastoring) is a huge responsibility before God. After all, according to the Bible each will be held accountable for their works. Still, we are not God. We are human. Humans err; and we know there are a small percentage of leaders that intentionally rob, steal, and mislead God's people for personal gain. There are even more that justify their lifestyles so freely they mislead and misguide others in their journey of justification. For this reason the truth admonishes us to be "grown-ups" in the Word. We are not to be like infants who do not understand the truth, hopping from one idea or teaching to another. We are to know what we believe and why we believe it. We are to be "steady" and unwavering in what we understand the Scriptures to teach us. Why do you believe this is vitally important for a believer?

_____

_____

_____

"Instead, speaking the truth in love, we will grow to become in every respect the mature body of him who is the head, that is, Christ." (Ephesians 4:15)

Again, this maturity factor is important to us who are striving to reach the goals God has before us. One goal reiterated here is love and unity. We need to be mature in our belief so we can speak the truths of the Bible. We also need to speak truth to ourselves and to others, most importantly speaking it in love. Have you ever been around someone who clearly knew the Scriptures well, yet they spoke to you in every manner other than love? How did that make you feel and why is our speech being seasoned with love so important?

_____

_____

_____

I know at times when I speak coarsely or harshly toward my children, their response is just that - coarse and hard! When I season my words with grace and love they always respond better. (They may not always obey, but that is another Bible study!) Our words and our attitudes definitely affect our atmosphere! If you want joy and peace in your home, speak with joy and peace on your lips.

Next, this idea of maturity and unity for the believers is necessary for the goal of being more like Christ. How can we become more like Christ if we do not learn more about Him? We have to act more like Him and less like "me." John 3:30 says, "He must increase, but I must decrease." (KJV)

This is the spiritual maturing process in a nutshell.

Finally, in this quest toward God's plans, goals, and works for us, we must once again see our part in the body of Christ as significant! When we understand the gifts and works God has laid before us for our lives are working toward maturity and unity in Christ, then we as a body or whole group of believers can accomplish so much more together for the Kingdom of God.

This "working together" is illustrated easily by thinking about our own bodies. Have you ever pulled a muscle in your back? Maybe stubbed a little toe? While these two examples may seem to have two extremely different affects upon the body, the little toe stub can be as debilitating as a pulled muscle in the back! No matter how small or insignificant you may feel, your part in the Body of Christ, maturing and growing in unity and love, joins us all together to do the magnificent works of God for the Kingdom. How can you encourage others in the body of Christ where you serve and worship to grow and mature in Christ?

_____

_____

_____

I have found when I focus upon God's work in my life I don't have time to focus on my struggles. What about you? How can finding God's plan and Kingdom work help you to overcome your struggles, hurts, or even dull-drums of in life?

Day 4 The Difference
Read Ephesians 4:17-24

The difference between our old selves before Jesus and our new selves in and through Christ is compared explicitly in these verses. The comparison is one we need to make fairly often in our walk with the Lord. I don't advise comparing ourselves to others or others' circumstances; it is just not healthy to compare in that way. Yet when done for a very specific purpose as outlined in these verses, it is a healthy practice and a guide to the goal of what God desires for each and every one of us. Yes, we are to compare ourselves to Christ! Our goal is to live by the Spirit of the Living God, who dwells within in us as believers. In verse 24 we are to "be like God." What does it look like to be like God? (HINT: The answer follows the phrase in verse 24-NLT)

We can only attain true righteousness and holiness or purity by the process of self-evaluation. To put it simply, we have to perform "a spiritual check-up." The verses say we are not to be a few things. How might we use verses 17-23 to give ourselves a spiritual check-up?

I've comprised a list of questions that may help in giving yourself a spiritual check-up. You can add to the list and expound upon it as you see fit, no pun intended!

1. Am I hopelessly confused about anything in my life?
2. Is my mind full of darkness and ungodly thoughts?
3. Is there any area of my life in which I have wandered away from God because I simply do not want to hear from God on that particular subject matter?
4. Do I have a sense of shame when I do wrong? Are there areas where I am calloused or hardened, where maybe I should feel shame and I do not?
5. Do I live for pleasure? ("Lustful" does not necessarily mean sexual lust as we might tend to assume in our current culture, but a strong desire.) You might think of it as a stronger desire for pleasure over contentment? Or possibly an unhealthy balance of something God may be tugging at your heart about?
6. Do I practice impurity of any sort in my life?

The Bible tells us to throw off any of these behaviors because they are remaining evidence of our old selves before Christ. Do not allow your mind to justify sin or lie to you by saying, "this is not so bad" or "you do not do that very often, you don't really have an issue with it." This is exactly what is meant at the end of verse 22 when it speaks about these lies "corrupting you through their lust and deception." Place your focus on the word "deception" here. How might deception be a huge "road block" to our ability to throw off our old selves and old behaviors?

Can you see how, as we exercise the spiritual self-check-up, we are naturally inclined to make ourselves sound like we do not have any issues with our old selves? The first thing I do when I start comparing myself to God's standard of righteousness and holiness is to deceive myself by telling myself I am not so bad, or what I deal with is ok because…. justification, justification, justification.

Can you name your justification? Deception is just as strong as our lust or our desire to be or do whatever we want to. Even dwelling on the hurts in our lives can deceive us just as much as any outward sinful act. Unfortunately, until we trade in our earth suits for a heavenly one, we will always need to make adjustments and alignments with our old selves and God's standard. Just as we need to have human physicals, we need to have spiritual physicals. Just as we need to align our tires on our vehicles, we need to align our minds, hearts, and behaviors with God. Unfortunately, this is not an easy task, nor a pleasant one. But God has not given us an impossible task. The great news is we can not only throw away our old suits daily, but also put on our new suits daily. More on this dressing up tomorrow!

Day 5 Put Off and Put On
Read Ephesians 4:25-32

What in life could be more appealing than wearing new clothes every day of our lives! I am not as big of a "fashionista" as my loving husband, but I do love to put on something new! Don't you? Today again we will be attempting to throw away some things in our old selves! While this is not the easiest task nor the most enjoyable topic to study, it is part of our spiritual walk and can become easier the more we "purge our closet," so to speak!

The passage has a lot of corrective rebuke within it. As we breeze through the Scripture study, try to think of it as taking a day to clean out your clothes closet! The great thing about purging out the clothes closet is we make room for the nice, new things God has in store for our lives. Depending on your personality, you may be the type that can pick and toss your clothes into that Goodwill bag without a care in the world. Others of you may be like me. I have to stop and consider if I might like to wear that item again. Will the styles cycle around again, or will I lose few pounds? Then my mind wanders to all the great times I have had wearing that piece of clothing before I eventually place it in the "maybe" pile!!! Just being brutally honest, some of us will have a harder time getting rid of our old selves than others. Please be patient with those of us that are more contemplative and possibly more strong-willed. As we go through these dos and don'ts, place a check mark beside the ones you really need to replace in your old self.

THROW AWAY PILE	NEW CLOTHES
Lying	Tell the truth
Don't be controlled by anger	Have self control
Quit stealing	Work hard and be generous
Quit foul or abusive language.	Be an encourager by letting everything you say be good and helpful
Don't bring sorrow to the Holy Spirit by how you live!	Remember what He did for you.
Get rid of bitterness, rage, anger, harsh words, slander and, in case we missed anything, all types of evil behavior!	Put on kindness

Let's review our new wardrobe:

1. TELL THE TRUTH
2. FORGIVE
3. WORK HARD AND BE A GIVER
4. BE AN ENCOURAGER
5. REMEMBER WHAT JESUS DID FOR YOU
6. BE KIND TO EACH OTHER!

How can we put on the new clothes? The "how" is built into the final verse, I believe. If we have a hard heart towards God, ignore His love, and forget what He has done for us, it will be very difficult to have a tender-heart toward others! The two are adamantly opposed to one another. A tenderhearted person is also going to follow through with the last part of the verse and be a forgiving person. When we constantly remember what Christ has done for us by forgiving us, we can then forgive others and be tenderhearted toward others.

How is your heart? Are you feeling cold and hard about what God is asking you to put off today? Which of the new clothes look the most appealing to you?

_____

_____

_____

Take time to simply reflect upon Jesus. Read again the Gospel of John. Meditate upon God's love through the story of His life. Scripture says "…God's kindness is intended to lead you to repentance." (Rom. 2:4b NIV) We can only be as sensitive to aligning our behaviors with God's standard as our hearts are tender toward Him.

I know tossing out those old clothes was not your idea of a day of fun. It was not my idea of a day of fun either! Still, how beautiful we will look in our new selves as we face our families and friends today!!

Week Six: Plans & Purposes
Ephesians 5:1-33

Key Passages: Imitate God, live a life filled with love, and carefully determine what the will of the Lord is.

Ephesians 5:1-2 (NIV)

> **"[1]Be imitators of God, therefore, as dearly loved children [2]and live a life of love, just as Christ loved us and gave himself up for us as a fragrant offering and sacrifice to God."**

Ephesians 5:10 (NIV)

> **"[10] and find out what pleases the Lord."**

My prayer is we each find our perfect path God wants for us, so we can know His plans and purposes for our lives. Psalm 32:8 is a verse I have been meditating upon for several months and it says, "I will instruct you and teach you in the way you should go; I will counsel you [who are willing to learn] with My eye upon you." (AMP)

This speaks volumes to me in that my path is made perfect as I follow my guide and listen for His advice. It is the best pathway. I believe God will not hide it from us. He doesn't sit on His throne, aloof when we seek to follow and hear Him. Yet, before we dive into knowing what pleases the Lord and making the most of every opportunity on days three and four, let's discover more of His extravagant love for us! We will finish up our week with a little self-evaluation because God has some strong words for us to consider in this chapter. We are getting near the end, so continue on and finish strong!

Day 1 Extravagant Love
Read Ephesians 5:1-4

As I prepared for this day of study, I remembered the road I was so privileged to walk several years ago. It was the main road down the ruins of Ephesus. One prominent memory from that leisurely stroll was the view of the library of Alexandria. At the very end of the first main street, the amazing architecture of the library draws you in, enticingly, as you walk ever so slowly along the streets of the downward sloping road. I recall vividly taking a little break from our walk through the ruins and sitting down catty-corner from the Library. It was no coincidence the city's brothel house was built right where we sat. I say it was no coincidence because the seductive women of the day knew where the men wealthy enough to pay for their time would spend their recreational hours.

As I was reading today's verses, I realized verse three mirrored this path and I wondered if the Apostle Paul remembered the downhill path straight into the brothel-library section of town?

The Message captures verse 4 of Ephesians this way: "Though some tongues just love the taste of gossip. Christians have better uses for language than that. Don't talk dirty or silly. That kind of talk doesn't fit our style. Thanksgiving is our dialect." (MSG)

Don't think for a minute those early Christians did not continue to rub shoulders with fellow citizens of Ephesus! Obviously, this city was full of sexual sin and all kinds of filthy practices that accompanied the city brothel. There is an interesting instruction here telling the believers to keep from gossiping. The NLT version calls this "obscene stories" Doesn't a local brothel and library make a great formula for gossip and obscene story telling? Well, add within a block of the library and brothel a bathhouse and bingo! You have yourself the perfect place to gossip about your neighbor and their neighbor for that matter. I am sure dirty talk and all kinds of foolish obscene conversations were the entertainment of each day as they gathered at the bathhouse. We can surely apply this to our culture with the instant and incredible technology of Social Media. We are wise to take note and check ourselves. We are to be a people who follow after Christ and model our lives after Him. We are to be like Him in our hearts, in our behaviors, and in our conversations. The Message says Christ's "love was not cautious but extravagant." (Eph. 5:1) He didn't love in order to get something from us but to give everything of Himself to us!!! Extravagant love is selfless, not self-seeking or promoting, a love that didn't "take" like that of the men who frequented the brothel of Ephesus. How the Apostle Paul's heart must have longed for these loose women to know the extravagant love of Jesus Christ. How can you check your gossip meter?

_____

_____

_____

A wise person once told me, "If the person you are taking information to about another person is not in a position to help, then the information is probably gossip." Another funny thing we do in the name of Jesus is we bring gossip up as a "prayer request." We try to justify our gossip by putting a spiritual label upon it. How this must churn God's stomach. Instead, how might we show extravagant love to those around us?

_____

_____

_____

Day 2 Getting Somewhere Fast!
Read Ephesians 5:5-8

As you can probably tell from the oxymoron of the title, God does not bless a life that is full of using others for personal gain. If you use people or anything for what you can get out of them or it, God calls this practice idolatry. The Scripture also has a lot to say about those who use faith like a "sales gimmick." I am not saying marketing or promotions for Sunday Series and the like are wrong. I am saying God knows our hearts! He sees those who make proclamation in the name of Jesus for their own personal gain, whether pride, position, or power: "God gets furious with people who are full of religious sales talk, but want nothing to do with him" (The Message Ephesians 5:6b)

The Bible says in the NLT that, "… an idolater is one who worships the things of this world." Ephesians 5:5b

I would not label very many people idol worshippers, but it is evident here we are in fact an idol worshippers if we are greedy people. In what form do we worship the things of this world through greed?

_____

_____

_____

While putting anything above God is idolatry and scary ground to tread upon, even worse is to fool ourselves into thinking we can justify or excuse this kind of ungodly behavior. In fact, in such happenings, the anger of God falls upon all who disobey Him in this manner.
 What do you think the anger of God looks like when it falls on someone today?

_____

_____

_____

One significant instruction here is to make sure all ties with those who are disobedient to God are broken. There is clear direction in Proverbs 13:20 those who walk with wise people (those who know right from wrong) are going to be wise themselves. However, those who are companions of fools will be fools. It does not state the fools will be fools, but as Christ followers who walk with foolish people, we will be the fools. This is a strong statement. Why would the believer be the fool instead of the one in darkness?

_____

_____

_____

The Apostle Paul states, "Once we were just like these idolatrous people, full of darkness, yet through Christ, we are now full of His light!"

We are called to live as "people of light;" so walk in light today. If you have an unhealthy relationship that produces the fruit of darkness in your life and is not a wellspring of life to those in darkness around you, what would it take to change?

_____

_____

_____

Day 3 What Pleases the Lord?
Read Ephesians 5:9-14

Today's verses challenge us as followers of the "Light" to produce only what is true, good, and right. This task must not be as easy as it seems when we simply read through the passage, because the very next instruction in the Word is to carefully determine what pleases the Lord. It would seem that determining what pleases the Lord should be easy right? I mean, are not daily choices right or wrong, black or white? LOL! We all know and understand every choice can be clouded with a shade of "gray." I remember a time when Paul and I had made a decision for him to take a position at a church in Tampa as a Youth Pastor. It was an easy black and right, no-brainer type decision - until we met with our current pastor. We were not on church staff at the time, but that pastor basically offered us a part-time position to stay at that church and work in ministry with them! Talk about mudding the water! The offer came out of left field and gave us something to think about for a day or two. We had to "carefully" determine what was going to please the Lord in that decision. Not all decisions are that weighty, but making hasty decisions just because they look and feel right may not be the decision that will ultimately please the Lord. So how do we carefully determine the Lord's will? Unless we are beguiled in an area of our lives, most behavioral decisions are easily decided upon by asking a simple question of the Lord.

"Is this pleasing to you, Lord?" A heartfelt question in our spirit will get an accurate response from God's Spirit. Gray areas may be a little more difficult to determine. Still, most of us must admit a question about a situation in our Spirit usually results in a "no" from God. We don't like to admit that a question will be answered with a "no" because we want to partake in the questionable activity and not feel the guilt we know will follow when we disappoint our Lord. I have definitely dabbled in questionable "no's" from God. Every time I need to justify my participation, my spirit senses God's disappointment in me.

Have you ever experienced a time when you sought the Lord for permission to dabble in a questionable area of your life and you knew while it was not an emphatic "no", it was still a gray decision? What did you do about it?

_____

_____

_____

Sometimes a "no" is a "no," and we can move on without much trouble. There is much instruction from God's Word about what is right and wrong in our lives, and on that we can stand firm. In these later verses, we are told to expose these dark practices. Yes, call them out for what they are! But those gray areas of life are the stumbling stones that easily trip us up! What are we to do with these gray areas?

I don't believe the Scripture is telling us to go into our communities and call out the darkness, but the instruction is more towards a practice of personal exposure. You see, when we hide behavior in our lives, especially questionable behaviors, we easily talk ourselves into justifying the behaviors as okay or even right. If we call our personal, private behavior out into the open, we can expose it for what it is. This may mean you tell someone else about it so it is really exposed! When we pretend God doesn't see it or even really care about, or when we say, "that's no big deal, really," we are in actuality trying to hide it from God. Our practice should be to shine God's light upon it and measure it against the Lord. If it is clean and right and true and good, as verse 9 states, then it is going to be pleasing to the Lord. However, when we shine the light of the Lord upon it and expose it, and comes up dirty or tainted in some form or fashion, we need to take that dirty laundry and wash it by the blood of Jesus and then hang it out to dry!

Is there any area of your life God is calling you to expose to the Light? How can you hang that dirty laundry out to dry?

_____

_____

_____

Sometimes life choices seem impossible. I am so thankful for faithful followers of Jesus that have left us with lifelong legacies we can aspire to live up to. A.W. Milne's (a one-way missionary to the New Hebrides Islands in the South Pacific) epitaph on his tombstone read: "When he came there was no light, when he left there was no darkness."[1] May this be our goal as we walk in this dark world.

Day 4 Opportunities
Read Ephesians 5:15-20

Yesterday we discussed gray areas of our lives. Today I want to continue bouncing around some thoughts about these areas of our lives and how they can affect God's will in us.

Today's key Scripture is one that is a favorite of mine: "Making the most of every opportunity." I think it is a favorite because it is a true challenge! I know there have been many days in my life I have made the most of every opportunity to serve the Lord, please Him, and do His will. However, I know there have been many more days in which I have missed an opportunity - sometimes every opportunity - to please the Lord. There have been grievous times of displeasing the Lord; I am certain of that fact. I know many of you have probably heard the illustration of the two dogs that war within us- our natural man and our spiritual man. They are likened to two dogs pulling a rope opposite directions from one another. The question is posed: which one wins the tug–o–war? Well, that is easily answered! It is the dog that gets fed the most!!

I love that illustration because it is a simple way to understand how important feeding is to our humanity. I love to eat, so I am thankful for the times of feeding my natural, physical body. Okay, I admit, I really love to eat! Yet feeding my spirit is even more important. Deuteronomy 8:1b and Matthew 4:4 says, "Man shall not live by bread alone but on every Word that comes from the mouth of God..." So which dog wins the tug-o-war in life? It is so much easier to make decisions to please the Lord, even in the gray areas of life, when we feed our spirit. It is so much easier to make the most of every opportunity that God presents to us in our lives when we are feeding the right dog! Some opportunities will not be seen, felt, or heard because they are spiritually discerned and only a well-fed spirit will be full enough to ascertain what the spiritual opportunity is. So how do we feed our spirit? We feed our spirit by every Word that comes from the Father's mouth. The Word of God feeds our spirit and makes us nutritionally fit so we can win the on-going battle over our natural man.

The study passage encourages us again today to seek what is the Lord's will. We are not to be foolish or be fooled ourselves. We are not to be drunk with wine but filled with the Spirit. I believe the comparison here is the exact scenario we have been talking about for two days. We are to expose (call out those things) in our lives that are not living up to the light of God and live in the spirit, not the natural realm. Yes, we eat, walk, and breathe in this earth-suit; but we are to be seeking the Lord's will and pleasing Him as we make the most of the spiritually discerned movements or opportunities in our lives. Our next command is to be filled with the spirit.

Today's verses tell us some ways to be filled with the Spirit. List them below:

1. _____

2. _____

3. _____

There is one more way to ensure we are properly pleasing God, but we will focus on that tomorrow.

Let us think about today's ways: speaking encouragement to one another, singing and making a song in our own hearts, and giving thanks are huge daily tasks. Let's jot down a few practical steps to show what these spirit- filling activities could look like in your everyday lives.

Encouraging one another

_____
_____
_____

Singing and making music in my heart

_____
_____
_____

Giving Thanks

_____

_____

_____

I believe as we feed our spirit through reading the Word, and as we practice these disciplines in our lives, we will see our spirit go from a malnourished state to a spirit-filled state. Then we will be able to make the most of every opportunity because we will be spiritually discerning and full to please the Lord and determine what His will is for your life.

Day 5 Submit, Really?
Read Ephesians 5:21-33

Submitting to those over me is not what I would pick to fill my spirit. Yet this is another step, like the previous three, we discovered in yesterday's study!

Maybe you can relate to this. I really hate to be told what to do and have rarely enjoyed being under someone else's authority. I would rather be the top dog. I teach school and this profession is great for me because I basically am the queen of my castle in that little classroom. For some reason God wired me this way and I know I am not the only one. However, there are times when I do want to be told what to do. Take shopping for example; when I am pressed for time and I have to buy a lot of items, I sometimes get stuck on whether or not to make a purchase. It may sound strange (and I am sure it is strange); but I get myself so worked up I even begin to have anxiety! The great news is God knows the way He has wired us! He knows me and I can rest in that fact. What I have done to remedy this little issue is to make my husband go with me and narrow down the purchases. Sometimes, I just tell him to get what he likes. This has been very freeing and really has cut down on my shopping expenditures. But mostly, it has freed me from feeling overwhelmed.

For the woman reading today's study has not been an easy task for some of you. If you are at all like me, you really may have grown to despise these words! I pray as we study along today you will see this message in a new light and God will work in you as He has in me. Some of you may love this passage of Scripture and you may already see the value and understand the heart of God in this matter. I pray you will be patient with the rest of us!

There is an old book written many years ago and as I mention the title many of you may think it must have been written in the Ice Age! It is "ME, obey Him?"[2]

This is the honest declaration all of us who are made female most assuredly have made or will make at some time in our lives. In fact, this age-old declaration goes all the way back to Genesis. Read Genesis 3:16

The curse is a curse indeed; but understanding the why behind it is important to our concern for why we need to obey our husbands.

Although it may make it easier to swallow knowing this is a result of the curse and not God's intended plan for us as women, still we live this curse and need to fully understand it.

It is obvious the pains that accompany childbirth are a part of the curse, but if we skip down to the desire part of the curse it calls into question a few ideas. Knowing men the way we do and how they are wired, it is not strange most men interpret this desire to mean we, as women, will want to have sex with them. But, as any woman in her right mind would think: How far from the truth is that? I mean, we do have desires for our husbands sexually, but not like that! The later part of that phrase continues and makes much more sense...."and he will rule over you." (Gen. 3:16b)

I believe that women desire to be the head as part of the curse! Yet, our husbands rule over us. Think about the conflicts that arise in your relationship. If we are honest, does it go back to you wanting to make a "better" decision than your husband? Maybe it is you wanting your desires to be over your husband's desires?

As much as I don't like it in my flesh - I can even say it just isn't fair and I know I am right more than he is right - this is God's decision, not mine. God is God, and I am not. Now, I am not saying we have to love it, but if you consider God and digest the following, you may come to like it!

Let me go back to my original little example of shopping. When I get overwhelmed with anxiety while shopping and I can't make a decision, it usually is rooted in whether or not I believe we have the finances to buy the item. So, in allowing my husband (who quite frankly has better taste than me anyway.... lucky me) to make the purchase, I take all anxiety out of the picture. Another example is, after 21 years of my keeping our finances in order, paying our bills and keeping track of what we had in our bank account, I passed that little puppy of responsibility over to my husband years ago. And I feel great. Because finances happen to be a source of frustration and anxiety to me personally, by giving the responsibility over to my husband, I have been freed from even "caring" about the bottom line of our accounts! I can buy free of care and worry. I can simply ask if I can spend and get an answer. Now that I have said all of this, I do recognize my gifting, abilities, and personality are all contributions to our relationship. Quite frankly, I am better at some things than my husband. Still, this is the concept of resting in obedience. There has been great security in trusting in my husband's good judgment. I am protected under his care, and I do not need to worry over what may happen because it is no longer my responsibility! Can you start to see how God has placed us as females in a secure place? We are free from the responsibilities of life because we are safe in our husband's care. Now his curse is to work by the sweat of his brow and bring in the food/finances! But God has us safely and securely under His ultimate care and watchful eye as we obey our husbands and as we honor and obey God because this is His plan for us.

Week Seven: Relationships
Ephesians 6:1-24

Key Passage: God's economy and protection in relationships
Ephesians 5:21-29 (NIV)

> "[21]Submit to one another out of reverence for Christ. [22]Wives, submit to your husbands as to the Lord. [23]For the husband is the head of the wife as Christ is the head of the church, his body, of which he is the Savior. [24]Now as the church submits to Christ, so also wives should submit to their husbands in everything. [25]Husbands, love your wives, just as Christ loved the church and gave himself up for her [26]to make her holy, cleansing her by the washing with water through the word, [27]and to present her to himself as a radiant church, without stain or wrinkle or any other blemish, but holy and blameless. [28]In this same way, husbands ought to love their wives as their own bodies. He who loves his wife loves himself. [29]After all, no one ever hated his own body, but he feeds and cares for it, just as Christ does the church"

In my book, I spent much of our time together sharing about the importance of our marital relationship. This week's study will emphasize the other important relationships in our lives and how God loves us and uses us to love others.

As we study together, may the Spirit of the living, loving God grant to you the experience of the fullness of God's love for you, for how great is His love for you. Be diligent in your study this week, Dear One.

Day 1 He Is the Owner
Read Ephesians 6:1-4

Absolutely love this passage of Scripture today. As a mother, I so want my children to grow up to know and love Jesus, and any Scripture that guides me into this outcome for my kids is especially near and dear to my heart. Honestly, I do not understand why the Lord only gave us a few verses of instruction here because I feel as if I need an entire book dedicated to instruction on raising kids! Yet the simple truths in these passages, if taught and caught by our children, will make a world of difference in their futures. One of the greatest reminders in verse 1 is our children belong to the Lord! I know we all quote this verse and we acknowledge it in our heads, but I know at times it is not deep in my heart. This knowledge gave me comfort when I lost our babies and a few years ago when pressed with the thought I might have to offer my boy back up to the Lord because of that bone cancer scare, I knew I didn't want to I felt "he is mine!" I cried to the Lord, even though I know he is God's child first. How do you reconcile the knowledge our children belong to the Lord with the feeling they are our own?

_____

_____

_____

I guess, like our finances, God is a much better owner and we are a better steward when we realize He is above all and overall and a much better Father than we could ever dream of being. God loves our children much more than we can imagine or fathom! We get the opportunity to manage and train and love them too, but HE is the Owner. The whole earth is His and everything in it! (Proverbs 89:11) This principle of ownership is vitally important to teach our children: it is not just that they are His, but the whole earth and everything in it is His too! Our world is so driven to clutch tightly in our hands our material possessions and goods. Modeling behavior that holds loosely to things of this world is one that will aid our kids in this materialistic-driven culture.

How might we show our children in practical ways that we are managers of all that is the Lord's in this world?

_____

_____

_____

As our kids understand to whom they belong, and as **we** fully grasp this idea deep within our hearts, we can also teach our kids that obeying and honoring us, as their parents given to them by God, will come with great rewards. What I mean by "great" here is this truth is a promise from God! The idea that lives will go well for us is incredible! However, there are even greater negative consequences on the opposite end of their choices.

What examples can you give where you have seen children grow up and experience negative consequences because of their disobedience and dishonor of their parents?

_____

_____

_____

Now, name those people that are living the fulfillment of God's promise of a life where "things have gone well for them."

_____

_____

_____

Verse 4 is one we need to pay particular attention as parents. It is vitally important to grasp this parenting skill, or should I say, forsake this parenting habit. I have seen in myself a tendency to respond and react in ways that bring anger out in my children. It usually is a result of my frustration being allowed to flow over recklessly to the point in which I feel agitated, stressed, and feelings of anger arise. Then these feelings bring a conversation to a boiling point in both my child and me! These types of "arguments" are full of angry outbursts, disrespectful judgments, and hasty generalizations. They rarely lead to a resolution of an issue but always bring about more strife and cause a wedge between us. That being confessed, when I experience times of patience, calmness, and peaceful confrontations, followed by consistency, we experience the fruits of peace in our relationship. And a much better resolve!

How might following a strategy to think through our feelings before confrontations and thus following a more peaceful and patient approach to parenting help you from falling into the trap of provoking your child to anger?

_____

_____

_____

What are some practical steps you can implement into your parenting today? Keep in mind recognizing what triggers your negative feelings and frustrations before they get too out of control will significantly aid in keeping yourself calm and collected as you give correction to your children.

_____

_____

_____

Day 2 Bound to Responsibilities!
Read Ephesians 6:5-9

I wonder if you experience what I feel oftentimes about the responsibilities of life. A wise friend and mentor once stated, "Raising children is like a life-sentence without the possibility of parole." Now that is harsh, but true. And as much as we all love our children and know they are a blessing from God, if we are honest with ourselves, we must admit the responsibility is life-long. Even when they are adults we still are bound to their successes, their families, their happiness, and we grieve when they grieve. If this is not being in a state of mental bondage of our own making, then I don't know what is. Another type of mental bondage is our careers. With most of our culture raising families in a one-parent household, or two-careered households, we are bound by our responsibilities at work. We have even placed unattainable expectations upon ourselves, and our families, when it comes to simply raising our kids. We have made ourselves bound to these impractical, unattainable expectations. If you have young children, you understand the idea of never having a moment to yourself. If you are in the season of life where you live in your car going from event to event for your kids, then you understand the emotional bondage that can accompany our busy lives. Being too busy is a type of bondage all wrapped up in an attractive bow that is really a deception of the enemy, but it screams to us, "This is required in order for you to be happy!" Yet, living this way leaves us tired, dissatisfied, and empty in our lives, much of the time. Where do you feel a type of mental bondage in your current season of life? Try to describe your feelings below:

_____

_____

_____

While we cannot fully understand what it meant to be a slave back in the Apostle Paul's day in Ephesus, we certainly can identify some of those times when we feel absolutely enslaved to responsibility! Whatever our state, the Bible has instruction for us. List a few goals for "how" we are to work and live under those who have authority over us? Whether our boss, or husband or whatever we do?

1. _____

2. _____

3. _____

4. _____

I am definitely NOT trying to add more to your plate! Nor am I trying to make you feel overwhelmed! We must trust in the blessings that will follow when we work in this manner, and it will result in a reward from the Lord!

I find it is quite difficult to do what anyone says with deep respect, fear, and sincerity. It is also difficult to please them all the time!

Working with enthusiasm is no small task and "with all of your heart"? As we focus on this work with the knowledge it is like a sacrificial offering and act of worship for the Lord, as we are working for the Lord instead of for people, the work seems a lot easier to accomplish.

As you think about your responsibilities, maybe some of us need to pray about backing away from some of the "stuff" in our lives that keeps us from being able to work whole-heartedly and with enthusiasm. I know I can only do a certain number of things well in my life. I am not one of those multi-tasking, gallon-sized women who are wired to do several things with excellence. God has created me to be able to handle more like a "pint-size" level of life's responsibilities.

Is there something you can cut out of your life today that would make you feel more free, rather than feeling like you are a bound to the responsibility?

_____
_____
_____

Day 3 The Dark Places
Read Ephesians 6:10-13

Have you ever had moments in your life you would label as "dark places"? I am talking about times when you felt alone or in despair. It could have been times of separation from those who you love. Some dark places are filled with fear you might lose someone you love. Other dark places can be identified with feelings of depression. I have felt dark places when I knew I was deep in sin and the guilt was ever present. I also have known dark places to be those filled with jealousy, strife, envy, bitterness, and even anger. Whatever the picture your dark places paint, be assured God is not the creator of our dark places. In fact, He tells us to bring to light those habits that are exercised in the dark places. We are to expose them. (Ephesians 5:11 KJV)

Through studying our passage today, I really want us to grasp the concept that dark places do exist. Even more importantly, we need to be aware of who inhabits the dark places. List the four main enemies with which we struggle in the dark places?

1. _____

2. _____

3. _____

4. _____

Since our struggles are not against what we see, but against **rulers**, **authorities**, **powers** and **evil forces that are spiritual**, how do we respond and prepare for the battles to come? This passage tells us to be prepared for battle by taking some action steps - put on the whole armor of God! We will study this important message tomorrow, but today we need to dig a little deeper into understanding our enemy. Any great warrior studies his enemy. We do ourselves a great disservice if we skip over this passage and assume we know the devil and his evil devices. So, let's pick apart these dark places and discover more so we can be as ready as any frontline warrior to take on the dark places in our lives. Because they are comin'! Be assured, they are comin'!

In my study of the "wiles" of the devil, a recurring word was prominent; the word is "deceive." If we can wrap our minds around this one description of the enemy's character – that of deceiver – we will be a step closer to understanding what our battle is against. Other prominent character descriptions of our enemy are as follows: cunning craftiness, patiently waiting for our demise, powerful in showing signs and wonders, and seductive. he is so good at deceit that he is able to transform himself into a beautiful "angel of light." In 2 Corinthians 11:14-15, we are warned the false prophet will be so close to the truth that many will be deceived. He beguiles his victims like he did to Eve. He lies! He prowls around seeking whom he can devour, like a roaring lion. He is not alone; fallen angels accompany his evil works.

These are just a few of the descriptions that I found in the Scriptures relating to the schemes or "wiles" of the devil. How can we filter these character traits into our thoughts so that we can ward off the enemy when he tries to devour us?

_____

_____

_____

Did you ponder the idea there is the possibility you are deceived about an area of your life? A telltale sign could be an area of your life you find yourself having to justify. I am not trying to be the Holy Spirit to anyone, because I know I have enough stuff in my life that needs adjusting. I have no platform to point fingers! Still, we are spiritually weak if we know our enemy's wiles, but do not take the necessary time to examine ourselves for weak areas where we may have fallen into deception.

It is imperative to understand the enemy's character in this preparation for battle but also the positioning, allowed by God, that our enemy holds.

There is an entire hierarchy of Satan and the fallen angels. It seems our passage today exemplifies the positioning and shows us where our enemy lives.

Supporting the concept of a hierarchy is the word "principalities," which is the descriptive word in the KJV. It is a Hebrew word with the root as "marashah." This Hebrew word's meaning is "Head place, at the head, dominion…the thing from which anything descends."[1] (Ephesians 6:12 KJV)

126

Also, in this study of the Hebrew language I found "spiritual wickedness" means wicked spirits. And "on high" literally means heavens or heavenly places.[2]

Not much other information is found on these four specific positions of our enemy, or I should say – "army" of enemies! Understanding what we are up against in this battle and with whom we are battling is a vital concept in our faith journey.

Supporting the idea of "many" in Satan's army is the use of plurals, such as "powers" and "rulers" which are literal words. Satan is the lord of this dark world, the one permitted by God Almighty to rule in this present darkness apart from God. In our sin, we experience a wicked ruler or authority who is reigning his dominion over us, as God allows us in our free will to make wrong choices. As an example, we can look at the negative power and authority one who is addicted to a controlled substance experiences. It is often while still under this power they realize the "stronghold" that binds them.

The best illustration that comes to my mind when considering a "stronghold" is the natural forces of gravity. Gravity is pulling to the earth. Like spiritual wickedness, evil forces are similar to gravity in that there is a strong pulling towards sin. Once snared, we are caught in the trap and cannot get out. This is the warning - Don't go there! Don't be trapped. Instead put on the armor of God!

Addiction is nothing more than one being under the authority and dominion of the evil ruler of this world! Once we are bound in his grip, don't think he is going to let go easily just because we whimper out a weak plea to be free! I know the grip a person addicted to drugs faces. These people go through months and even years of battling the pull that drug holds on them.

I am not saying we can't be free, but I do want to convey clearly what we take so often for granted – that we could be walking around under the rule and authority of spiritual wickedness and not even know it! If every time you get frustrated you let out an angry outburst, Satan doesn't need to get you to take drugs or into some other form of addiction. You are already under his authority in the area of self-control. This kind of living in the dominion of evil and serving that lord, because whether or not you realize it, you are damaging your family and especially your kids. I see the pattern of anger already in my children. I know what a battle it is to keep a calm disposition in the midst of the battle; I know what it is to win and to lose it literally lose it! I have walked down the path of justifying it as being "just who I am, or part of my personality." "I am just spirited and passionate!" I have lied to myself. When the enemy of our souls lies to us, we take up the lie and use it on ourselves. My best self-soothing device is to assure myself "I cannot change this area of my life without God's help, so God will give me grace and forgiveness." While that is a fact of truth, the consequences are grave.

So now I have shared my battles, what area of your life are you lying to yourself about? Can you ask God to reveal the truth about it? Is there any area of your life you can identify the pull of "evil forces" working?

_____

_____

_____

What do you feel the Spirit of God is telling you in this moment as we try to decipher the evil?

_____

_____

_____

We have a long battle ahead of us in this life…take heart; we already know WHO has won the war! And we are His and He is ours!

Day 4 Battle Gear
Read Ephesians 6:13-17

"Battle Gear!" I love the title of this lesson; it makes me feel like I am getting ready to play a video game. Unfortunately, life is not a video game and is played in living color with all the reality the enemy can muster up to trip us up! So we must prepare ourselves for battle. The amazing thing about preparing for battle is we all prepare differently. We each have different weaknesses and flaws, and need different battle plans. Our enemy attacks us differently. He knows us better than we know ourselves. Still, the awesome truth is we will win if we follow the instruction plans in verse 13! What are two imperative commands as we go to battle according to verse 13?

1. _____

2. _____

Put on every piece of armor and resist the devil! What a great God we call not only our Father, but also our Commander and Chief! We take on our responsibility and He holds up His end of the deal. When we do our part we can only call God a liar if we do not win our battle. Have you ever thought maybe you have not put on every piece of armor? Maybe there is a part of you that simply did not resist the enemy? Sometimes it is just easier to give in, I admit it! Sometimes we just need to admit we have a "chink" in our armor.

So what are these armor pieces with which we must prepare ourselves? We find a belt, body armor, shoes, a shield, a helmet, and, lastly, a sword.

Since we are preparing for a "spiritual battle," not a battle of literal flesh and blood as evidenced in the studied Scriptures yesterday, in the following spaces write what the "spiritual" relationship to each piece of armor is and how we must prepare ourselves.

1. BELT

_____
_____
_____

2. BODY ARMOR

_____

_____

_____

3. SHOES

_____

_____

_____

4. SHIELD

_____

_____

_____

5. HELMET

_____

_____

_____

6. SWORD

_____

_____

_____

Each piece of our armor should make us think in applicable terms as we prepare for whatever the enemy sends our way each day. So, as we consider each piece, how can we daily apply this battle plan to our lives? Give at least one practical example for you.

_____

_____

_____

For me, I have a battle plan preparedness checklist. It goes as follows: Check for truth/belt. I know the deceiver will start a little white lie or a seemingly innocent thought that is not blatant but is a statement that could be true about me or could be true about my current situation. For me putting on the belt of truth is stating facts that are true to combat the little white lies of the enemy. I only find this truth in knowing what God says about me through His Word, not focusing on how I feel about myself that particular moment. My feelings fail me almost every time, but the Word is constant and faithful.

My next check in my battle preparedness plan is to check for righteousness/body armor. I ask myself the question, "Am I right with God?" I know in myself, I cannot be righteous, but according to Romans 7:17, "For if, by the trespass of the one man, death reigned through that one man, how much more will those who receive God's abundant provision of grace and of the gift of righteousness reign in life through the one man, Jesus Christ."
Because of Christ, we can boldly state, "I am the righteousness of God through Christ!" Therefore, am I right? So, I search myself for any area of unconfessed sin or tainted flaws in my body armor and ask myself, "Am I right with God?"

Next, I check for peace/shoes. What is my daily agenda? Does it include God? Am I ready to be a light to the dark world with the peace that only comes through knowing Jesus? Is my atmosphere, whether home or away, a sphere of peace or turmoil? Is it a place where the Gospel can be sown and cultivated so that I am ready to give at a moment's notice the Answer – Jesus, who is the peace that passes all understanding.

Another check is the important faith check! Am I walking by faith or by what is seen? Is there any God experiences I may be missing by living just to accomplish my daily agenda? Many times I know the enemy doesn't need to throw any "fiery darts" at me because I am so earthly minded I don't even consider my walk of faith. I am so driven to accomplish the "to-do list" that I don't give thought to a divine appointment making its way into my mundane daily routine! This is convicting to me as I am writing this because it is a revelation showing how much I am hunkering down in the fort of the routine of life instead of ambushing life with faith! Am I hoping for God to show up every day and believing the unseen hand of God is working in my life and in those around me? Check it off? Faith walk?

Next, I need to check my salvation meter. Have I thanked God for saving me today? Have I acknowledged His power at each finger's disposal because I am His and He is mine? When the enemy is raging a battle upon me, whether in my mind or through physical circumstances, do I have my solid helmet of salvation assuring me whatever happens I am His and He loves me this much? In this knowledge my battle is already won and I can never cower under the enemy's evil devices.

Finally, the Spirit/sword check is in order. Have I spent time in the Word of God so the Word of God, which summons the Spirit of God to act on my behalf, will move? The Spirit is our reminder, but if I haven't memorized anything deep within my mind and heart, then the Spirit will have few defenses to bring to my mind. It is the Word that is alive and powerful and active in our lives, not a devotional book, self-help website, or even words of Godly mentors. If I have not spent time meditating on the Word of God and specifically those Words of God I know I need for my specific weaknesses and flaws, then how can I ever be prepared for battle?

In considering the armor of God, is there a piece you recognize as a "weak link" in your armor? List it now and write a resolution to strengthen it.

_____

_____

_____

Day 5 Pray
Read Ephesians 6:18-24

It would be an understatement to say we need to pray. We do not only need to pray; we must pray. We are to pray at all times, in all situations, on every occasion, in every season of life! When I last studied the words "all" I believe I came up with the powerful conclusion, "all" meant all! So, when do we stop praying? We never stop praying. Prayer is our closest connection to God. Because of Jesus, we are told we can "Come boldly to the throne of God." (Hebrews 4:16 NLT) We no longer need a High Priest to go into the Temple and give a sacrifice for us like was needed in the Old Testament. Nor do we need a mediator to go before God Almighty and bring our petitions. Since Jesus, we can boldly and without fear come before God!

How much time do you spend in a day praying?

Circle One: Never - - Very Little - -When In Need - -Some Time - -A Lot!

The next part of the verse in Ephesians 6:18 tells us to "Be alert!" We are to watch with a purpose and perseverance.

Why do you think we are admonished so strongly to be alert, when we were just given our military preparedness orders in the previous verses?

_____

_____

_____

We are dumb sheep! God knows we forget and we are lazy! He knows we are not as intelligent as we hope we are! I know if I am not reminded, I can easily fall into my old routine of waking up and considering me and only me! The entire rest of the chapter encourages us, the believers, to not only pray for ourselves but also to pray for others. We are such a needy people!! We need direction, and God gives it. I pray this study has stretched your faith and your relationship with God our Father. I pray you will be bold as you walk in peace and follow the path of faith God has purposed for you. I pray each and every day you live out loud His calling upon your life and the losses in your life will be healed!!! I pray you will be a "healer" to others who are hurting and with the Word as our protector, you will know you are deeply loved.

Today's homework is to make a list you will be willing to pray over every day for a week. Don't forget to add things for which you are thankful as well as needs and requests.

_____

_____

_____

_____

_____

_____

_____

Week Eight: Peace Principle and Love Edict
Romans 8:28-32

Key Passage: All things work together for the good in God's purposes and plans for those that are in Christ Jesus!
Romans 8:28

> **"28And we know that in all things God works for the good of those who love him, who have been called according to his purpose."**

Through the long medical road with Anthony, one constant remained in our hearts. This constant was the peace of God. It truly was a peace that surpassed all understanding. I am so thankful for His peace.

As we study together, may the Spirit of the living, loving God grant to you the experience of the fullness of God's love for you, for how great is His extravagant love for you. Stick it out to the end, my friend, because this is an important week

Day 1 Reassurance God Loves Me This Much
Read Romans 8:28-32

I realize this is a review from our earlier weeks. Still, I want to make sure our hearts are assured and reassured of the fact God truly does LOVE US THIS MUCH! Even in the midst of our fear, God loves me this much. Even in the possibilities of pain and loss, God loves me this much. Even in the middle of Anthony's life-threatening scare of bone cancer, God loved me this much. Whatever you are going through today, God loves you this much. Even when you are angry with God, He loves you this much. While the passage in Ephesians teaches us how much God loves us, the passage in Romans teaches that we can never be separated from His great love. Romans 8 lists some scary and hurtful things could cause us to waiver in our belief that God loves us this much. Some of these faith stealers are: trouble, calamity, persecution, hunger, becoming destitute, danger, being threatened with death.

With our beloved son Anthony, our real threat was death. Even in the threat of death, even when I didn't feel His love, God still loved me.

What assurance do you need today to know God does love you and nothing can separate you from His love? Is there some trouble in your life? Are you experiencing calamity? What about persecution? Persecution can come in several forms: persecution at work for your faith in Christ, persecution at school, or even physical persecution. Many believers in Jesus are physically persecuted for their faith all over the world. Are you suffering financially? What about dangers in your world? Finally, for all of us, we will experience the threat of death. We are all terminal, you know? Still, the threat of death is difficult to swallow especially when it comes to those who are too young to die. Since writing this study, a friend passed away a few days past her 38th birthday. Although I didn't know her long, God granted me the opportunity to witness a woman, full of grace, walk through her final battle with cancer with love and faith for her God. She made the most of every opportunity to please her Lord, and she overflowed with this love as she talked to others as well as she walked it. Grieving her loss reminded me of the way God spared our son, and every day I try to remember to thank Jesus for giving us favor and healing with Anthony.

Can you think of a time you were or are afraid of death?

Do you need to be assured God loves you and nothing will ever separate you from His love for you? If so, what Scriptures come to mind from our study?

_____

_____

_____

Day 2 Am I Prepared for the "All Things?"
Read Romans 8:28-39

It seems trite to encompass the most hurtful experiences in our lives with a summation of a few verses in Romans. I guess that is one reason why this chapter was left until the study was almost completed. I pray through the study of the Word and sharing our stories together we can really see God's love for us in "all things."

Still, after weeks of study in Ephesians and a life of being raised in church and around authentic Godly examples of Jesus, nothing prepared me for the ordeal we walked through with our son, Anthony. It was the scariest time in my life so far. That phone call that drives you to your knees is never easy; I don't care who you are. What I believe with all my heart is as we learn to walk with Jesus, drill His Word into our hearts, and make preparations for spiritual battles so we are prepared for the "all things" in our lives.

What about you? How prepared are you for the "all things"?

List a few solid statements you can verbalize in times of need. I have given you a starter, but feel free to write anything God speaks to your heart.

I believe

_____

_____

_____

God says

_____

_____

_____

Because He loves me this much, I can

Day 3 Reflection of the Study

Before we get to your reflection, I cannot allow the nagging question that drove me to this end, a study in the book of Ephesians and the candid look into my life, go unanswered without emphatically restating it one last time. "God must have made mistakes in my life, or He really must not love me very much?" Please indulge me for a final study of this area of my life.

Well, let's quickly look at the dictionary definition of **mistake**[1]

   –noun

   1.   an error in action, calculation, opinion, or judgment caused by poor reasoning, carelessness, insufficient knowledge, etc.

   2.   a misunderstanding or misconception.

   –verb (used with object)

   3.   to regard or identify wrongly as something or someone else

   4.   to understand, interpret, or evaluate wrongly; misunderstand; misinterpret.

   –verb (used without object)

   5.   to be in error.[2]

So, Does God Make Mistakes? With a glance at the dictionary definition of mistake, I would say an emphatic no! God does not make mistakes. However, I have made mistakes in misunderstanding the love and character of God and misinterpreting His perfect plan for my life as something other than His perfect plan for my life.

Can God error? Whether in action, calculation, opinion, or judgment? Is God careless or insufficient in knowledge? Could God interpret, or evaluate wrongly?

Again, emphatically no! God is perfect in action, calculation, opinion, and judgment. He is the all-knowing, the brightest and the best at interpretation because His purposes and plans trump all of our understanding and minutest knowledge of Him.

These questions challenged all understanding and conception I had of God at the time. I even justified the thought He could choose to make a mistake, if He so desired, because He is God. The Bible says in I Cor. 2:10-11, Matt.11:27, Job 9:4, He is all-knowing, all-powerful, omniscient…HE is all of these and more. The Bible also states, "He never slumbers nor sleeps." (Psalm 121:3 ASV)

Since God is God and I am not, I am learning I need to trust in what I know about God…His character and particularly His faithfulness and unconditional love, and not forgetting HIS Word as the imperative point where I am learning to place my trust.

What I have learned and I pray you have as well is I was chosen long before time to be all God wants for me to be with works He has designed especially and specifically for me. So as a dear, daughter of the King, I have to be ready and alert to these wonderfully chosen assignments.

So, today as I have reminded myself of what I believe and why, now it is your turn. I would love for you to pick several passages from Ephesians and as the Holy Spirit directs you, meditate upon the verses and write down what God is speaking to you, as you reflect on all we have shared and studied together in His Word. I love you and God loves you this much!

_____
_____
_____
_____
_____
_____
_____
_____
_____
_____
_____
_____
_____
_____
_____
_____

Day 4 What Is a Love Edict?

God has beautifully written a love letter to us through His word. As we conclude our study time together, I believe one last exercise will begin to draw together all God has for us in understanding and experiencing His extravagant love for us in this life and the life to come. This is a personal exercise. Sometimes nothing moves our cold hearts like singing a song and replacing the third person pronouns with our own names. If you have never sung a song in this way try it. It is humbling immediately and it strikes down any pride left from our innate desire to be self-preserving and independent of God. Try it? Pick any song you know. For example, try David Crowder's song, "How He Loves."[3] Just sing the chorus aloud and insert your name, or pick a song of your own.

"Oh how He loves (your name here) so, Oh how He loves (your name) How He loves (your name) so. Oh He loves (your name) oh how He loves (your name) Oh how He loves (your name) Oh how He loves!"[4]

Now we are going to write a letter from God to us expressing all the ways He loves us. Make sure to make it personal. Go back over the last several days if you need to get ideas of how God loves you in your life. Be specific and use your name. (I have some examples of love edicts my girls wrote at the end of our Ephesians study together and they have allowed me to share with you their love edicts.

Dear Daughter,

You tend to wonder how in the world I could possibly LOVE you so, given your humanity. But I created your humanity, and you are the unique work of My hands. When I look on you, I see the precious, costly blood of your Savior, my Son Jesus. His blood covers you, as does my limitless grace. So breathe deeply, and often, taking in the reminder for how I have lavished my grace on you, along with my wisdom and understanding. You would do well to remember tis daily.

And having REDEEMED you, I have made you alive in Christ. And to prove this, I have given my Holy Spirit to live in you. It is my Holy Spirit who will guide you to make correct decisions and give you access to me. Let Him rule in you so that you will have peace. I want this for you.

And be careful to avail yourself of the complete armor that I have given you while you walk the earth. You'll need it to fight the battles that are sure to come your way. I will fight for you, but come dressed to the battle -be smart.

Oh, and your beloved husband is my gift to you. Respect him and I'll admonish him to love you. That's my job, so leave it to me.

So rest in my love; it is too deep for you to fully comprehend. Just trust me when I tell you that you are my beloved. And if you'll just love me back, fully and without reservation, walking in obedience, I will be pleased.

Love,
Your Loving Eternal Father

Oh Daugher,

We have walked together for years, some strong and sturdy and others on shaky ground. When you opened your heart, I was there. I was even with you when you turned away. Through the years you should know that I have big plans for you. As long as you continue to have faith in me and follow the guidance I have provided, I will continue to show you truth and bring blessings to you and your family.

You are a wonderful mother and wife. Look how well your family has grown and flourished. You guided your husband to become the man he was destined to be. See how well he leads and provides for your family. That comes from your obedience and submission. You have raised your children to be a blessing, and not strife to others and that is exactly what they are becoming. Continue to pray over them and lead them toward me.

Although you feel you have fallen short, keep your hope up and your eyes on the path and I will give you peace and strength to overcome any turmoil that you may face in the future. I know you have this strength in you already just don't be afraid and stay strong and grounded in the truths you already know.

I am so proud of what you have accomplished in life so far. I look forward to seeing what you continue to do. I know it will be just as great.

I love you this much!
God

Now that you have read some examples of daughters loved by God, go ahead with your edict. I will help you start

Dear _____

DAY 5 Your Love Edict

TODAY take your love edict and read it out loud to yourself. Make any adjustments or modifications. A lot can happen in a 24 hour time period. Keep this letter somewhere close so you can pull it out anytime you need to be reminded God loves you this much! I would love for you to take your love edict to your group and share it if you feel you can. However, if you cannot share it, know God is not the only one that loves you, dear friend. As we end our journey together, there is one more thing about me I want to share with you. The struggle between what I know in my head and what I believe in my heart continues. This battle is often a daily fight. If I do not intentionally take time to align my heart with the truth of God's word and God, I may find myself along the dark path that goes against the truth.

This struggle is my struggle; yet, I believe we all can understand how important it is to walk with God and align our hearts with Him every day. Whatever your struggle, I pray you take the truths of God's love for you and stomp out the lies of the enemy who is like a roaring lion seeking whom he may devour!

Finally, I truly want to thank you for allowing me to speak into your life. I pray the Lord bless you and keep you. The Lord will make His face to shine upon you, and give you peace. (Numbers 6:24-26)

Always remember Dear One,
God loves you this much!

Acknowledgments

This work would not have been possible without the emotional and prayer support of my family and close friends. I am especially indebted to Lee Sullivan, for her extensive professional guidance and tireless hours to formatting both books. She has been supportive of my writing, and a huge encouragement in completing these books.

I am grateful to all of those with whom I have had the pleasure to work during this project. I also want to thank Josiah and Hannah Siegmund, who also provided many hours in editing the workbook.

Notes

Week One – My Song

1. Spurgeon, Charles. The Spurgeon Archive. (http://www.spurgeon.org/sermons/2266.htm)
2. Stott, John R. W.   The Message of Ephesians John R. W. Stott Inter Varsity Press 1989
3. Ibid.
4. Guzik, David. "Commentary on Ephesians 1". David Guzik's Commentaries on the Bible." http://classic.studylight.org/com/guz/view.cgi?book=eph&chapter=0011997-2003

Week Four – Sugar & Spice

1. Schindler's List, directed by Stephen Spielberg, scripted by Steven Zaillian, MCA, 1993.
2. Boyd, Aaron, "God of This City" Greater Things, Label Bluetree, September 2007.
3. Supercalifragilisticexpialidocious Performed by: Mary Poppins (Julie Andrews) Written by: Richard M. Sherman and Robert B. Sherman.

Week Six – Plans & Purposes

1. A.W. Milne was one: From a lecture by Dr. Howard Foltz, a missiology professor at Regent University, 2002.
2. Rice, Elizabeth Hanford. "Me Obey Him" Latest Publication Amazon.com 2005.
3. Blue Letter Bible Lexicon https://www.blueletterbible.org/lang/lexicon/lexicon.cfm?Strongs=H4761
4. Ibid.

Week 8 – Peace Principle & Love Edict

1. "mistake." Dictionary.com. 2017. https://www.dictionary.com (5 August 2017)
2. Ibid.
3. John Mark McMillan, "How He Loves" The Song Inside: The Sounds of Breaking Down. Label, John Mark McMillan, November 2005.
4. Ibid.

Made in the USA
Columbia, SC
24 August 2017